TUPAC SHAKUR

Tupac Shakur

THE LIFE AND TIMES OF AN AMERICAN ICON

TAYANNAH LEE MCQUILLAR

&

FRED JOHNSON, PH.D.

DACAPO PRESS
A MEMBER OF THE PERSEUS BOOKS GROUP

Set in 10.5 point Arno Pro by the Perseus Books Group

Library of Congress Cataloging-in-Publication Data

McQuillar, Tayannah Lee, 1977–
  Tupac Shakur : the life and times of an American icon / by Tayannah Lee
McQuillar and Fred Johnson. — 1st Da Capo Press ed.
    p. cm.
  Includes bibliographical references and index.
  ISBN 978-1-56858-387-7 (alk. paper)
  1. Shakur, Tupac, 1971-1996. 2. Rap musicians—United States—
Biography. I. Johnson, Freddie Lee. II. Title.
  ML420.S529M37 2010
  782.421649092—dc22
  [B]
                    2009040299

First Da Capo Press edition 2010

Published by Da Capo Press
A Member of the Perseus Books Group
www.dacapopress.com

Da Capo Press books are available at special discounts for bulk purchases in
the U.S. by corporations, institutions, and other organizations. For more
information, please contact the Special Markets Department at the Perseus
Books Group, 2300 Chestnut Street, Suite 200, Philadelphia, PA 19103, or call
(800) 810-4145, ext. 5000, or e-mail special.markets@perseusbooks.com.

10 9 8 7 6 5 4

Hip-hop's greatest gift and its heaviest burden—is its legacy of urban mythology. It will be remembered as that bittersweet moment when young black men captured the ears of America and defined themselves on their own terms. . . . In doing so, they raised a defiant middle finger to a history that shamed them with slavery, misrepresented them as coons and criminals, and co-opted the best of their culture.

—JOAN MORGAN
Vibe MAGAZINE
OCTOBER 1995

CONTENTS

STAR

· part four ·
AVENGER

· part five ·
BELOVED

part one

SAVIOR

one

THE BOY FROM NOWHERE

e was fifteen years old. His life had been a series of new addresses, hunger pangs, political meetings, and scary questions from FBI agents. Since early childhood, he had fought hard to survive.

He wrote poetry about love, life, and loneliness. He called himself MC New York and dreamed of someday becoming a rap star.

He came from nothing and nowhere. It was 1986 and a terrible war was being waged upon the poor in Tupac Shakur's America. He was always broke and kids teased him about his strange name and ragged clothes. He learned to use fake bravado and refined his skills on the microphone to make his peers like or at least respect him.

He hung out with his friends, bought marijuana for his mother, and stayed at his friend John's house whenever he could. John was a wealthy white boy who used to attend Tupac's school. There was always food at John's house.

Tupac Shakur's life was a rags-to-riches saga with elements of loneliness, cowardice, generosity, delusion, courage, humiliation, celebrity,
and a lifelong quest for family approval. It began in Lumberton, North
Carolina.

two

LUMBERTON

Growing up, Tupac Shakur heard much about the Lumbee Indians of Lumberton, North Carolina. They were alleged to be the only Native Americans to wage war against the Ku Klux Klan and win. Tupac's maternal ancestors came from Lumberton.

Founded by an act of the North Carolina General Assembly in 1787, Lumberton was the Robeson County seat. It had been established in 1787 in honor of Colonel Thomas Robeson, who'd fought in the Revolutionary War at the battle of Elizabethtown and defeated the British sympathizers.

When Lumberton was incorporated, the section of the Lumber River where it was located was known as Drowning Creek. Lumber and naval supplies were shipped from there. The city's economic development was based on lumbering, tobacco curing, textile and apparel manufacturing, and farm produce.

In the 1730s when Anglos from the Scottish Highlands settled in the area, they found local inhabitants who were the descendants of Native American ethnic groups like the Tuscarora, Cherokee, and Chera. A few spoke English as a result of contact with English settlers during the colonial period. That contact had often been characterized by suspicion and conflict.

Area Native Americans consistently resisted injustice and harassment. For example, in 1715 the Yamasee people led a mass uprising against the English who'd been their one-time allies in a war against the Tuscaroras. The source of conflict had been the breakdown in trade relations with the whites, and this, among other things, resulted in the Yamasees becoming dependent upon European goods and the steady loss of their ancestral lands. Attempts by colonial authorities to force the Yamasees onto reservations as well as Yamasee anger at their reduction to peonage produced warfare on April 15, 1715.

Fighting alongside the Yamasee, at least for a moment, were the Creeks, Choctaws, and Cherokees. But Cherokee dependence on European goods and cultural affinity eventually ruined the Native American alliance. The Yamasee and their allies fled, opening up more land for European settlement.

By the time the Scots Irish settled into the area of the Lumber River, the region had seen its fair share of conflict between Native Americans and European settlers for land and resources. Those Scots Irish settlers also found among the Native Americans of both freed blacks and runaway slaves.

When the American Civil War broke out in 1861, Native Americans, blacks, and whites had spent years in troubled coexistence. The tension boiled over during what became known as the Lowry War in 1865.

Stories pertaining to the Lowry War held that seventeen-year-old Henry Berry Lowry witnessed the execution of his father, Allen Lowry, and his brother, William, by the Confederate home guard. They had been suspected of leading a gang that had evaded authorities seeking to dragoon them into working hard labor for the Confederacy.

The men and their followers hid in swamps and eventually staged a series of raids on wealthy planters. The Confederate home guard, a type of local militia, searched farms and homes on March 3, 1865; they found stolen guns, clothes, and other items at Allen Lowry's home. He was subsequently arrested along with his wife and five of their twelve children.

In the hastily convened "trial" that followed, two of Allen Lowry's sons, Calvin and Sinclair, were acquitted since no stolen items had been found on them. Their brother William tried to escape but he was eventually executed along with his father.

Henry Berry Lowry watched the proceedings from a nearby thicket and resolved to seek revenge. The young Native American marshaled his black and Indian supporters and they waged a seven-year campaign of guerrilla war, raiding and harassing wealthy elites and outfoxing local law enforcement.

For the poor communities of impoverished and harassed Native Americans, blacks, and even poor whites, Henry Lowry and his raiders became heroes. Lowry and his followers came to symbolize the power of the powerless to resist those who preferred that they quietly endure their small worlds of blight and misery.

Perhaps it was the courage of the Lumbee Indians and Henry Lowry that encouraged other citizens to stand their ground and fight against bigotry and injustice.

In the late 1890s, Tupac's great-great grandfather, a dirt-poor white man from Lumberton who went by the name of Powell, married a black woman named Millie Ann. As punishment, his family tied him to a wagon, dragged him through Lumberton, and never spoke to him again. Millie Ann was religious and walked the dusty roads of Lumberton singing gospel music and reading Bible verses from door to door.

By the end of the 1920s, Powell's family and most southerners were faring poorly. Charles J. Shields, author of *Mockingbird,* noted that "the cultural index, or standard of living, in the South at the end of the 1920s was already the lowest in the nation. The region was at the bottom of the list in almost everything: ownership of automobiles, radios, residence telephones; income per capita; bank deposits; homes with electricity, running water, and indoor plumbing. Its residents subscribed to the fewest magazines and newspapers, read the fewest books; they also provided the least support for education, public libraries and art museums."

As the twentieth century progressed, discontent in the face of southern racism simmered in Lumberton's impoverished black community and among Native Americans. Tupac's mother, Alice Faye Williams, a great-granddaughter of Powell and Millie Ann, was born in Lumberton into this atmosphere of conflict and resistance on January 10, 1947.

By 1958, the Native Americans and blacks in Lumberton finally decided that it was time to stand up to their detractors. As in the past, African Americans and Native Americans fought side by side. On January 13, 1958, they battled Lumberton's Ku Klux Klan and drove the terrorist group out of town. Tupac's mother spoke about the incident in *Afeni Shakur: Evolution of a Revolutionary,* a biography by Jasmine Guy. She said, "The Lumbee didn't take no shit from white folks. . . . Klan came in and tried to impose a ten o'clock curfew on the Indian and Black community. Posted notices up about race mixing and basically wanted to control the Lumbees and treat them like niggers. So the Klan had a rally posted—the time and place and everything. Well, the Lumbees got guns and rifles and ambushed the Klan at their own rally. . . . Those white-hooded crackers ran into the woods like the little wing wangs they were. . . . That was my first taste of resistance."

During Tupac Shakur's lifetime, anyone who wondered about the origins of his commitment to social justice and his willingness to assist those in need had only to look to the marginalized citizens of his ancestral home of Lumberton and their traditions. Blacks from the area, including his mother, delighted in telling their children about the courage and heroism of the Lumbee Indians and how they had success-fully bested their oppressors. As children, Tupac and his sister, Sekyiwa, heard the Lumbee tales that had been passed down from generation to generation.

three

ALICE

Although Tupac's maternal grandmother, Rosa Belle Williams, wanted to stay in her hometown of Lumberton, her husband Walter insisted that they move to Norfolk, Virginia, where he had been born. Their first child was a girl they named Gloria. Their second child, Alice Faye, was born in Lumberton while Rosa Belle was there visiting a sick relative.

Alice Williams spent the first part of her childhood in Norfolk, Virginia, where Walter supported his wife and two daughters as a truck driver. When Walter refused to follow in the path of his preacher father, the elder man cast him out and forced other family members to do the same. Undaunted, he tried to join the Navy but his flat feet disqualified him. In addition, Walter, like every other southern black man of the time faced daily humiliation due to racist laws and customs. It is not possible to know if a combination of family alienation, dashed career goals and racism turned Walter into a wife beater. Perhaps he was just plain mean. Whatever the case, Rosa Belle paid a brutal physical price for his emotional problems.

From 1910 to 1920, Norfolk's population grew from approximately 67,000 people to nearly 116,000 due to the influx of newcomers seeking work at recently established manufacturing plants. By 1922, Norfolk had strengthened its economic position with the establishment of a $5 million grain elevator and terminal and a $500,000 farmers' market.

By 1940, the population of Norfolk, Virginia, had grown to 144,000. World War II produced another growth spurt for Norfolk as thousands of workers flocked to the city to work in the massive arms industry. From 1940 to 1944, the city's population swelled and there was rapid growth in furniture manufacturing, fertilizer plants, and other products. For Norfolk's black citizens, however, life was limited to the segregated Jim Crow South.

Racism and segregation maintained a stranglehold on life for blacks. For example, in 1968 the state of Virginia still considered interracial marriages a felony. That status was finally challenged and overturned in the Supreme Court case of *Love v. State of Virginia*. And although Norfolk hired its first black police officers in 1945, racism remained an unmistakable element in the city's social environs.

In the midst of such hardship, Alice Faye Williams grew up in a household that was additionally stressed as her father neglected the family and repeatedly beat her mother. "We were all poor," Alice recalled. "In fact, that is what held us together as a community. Like our neighbor, Miss Hattie. This lady liked my mama, and she knew our situation. You didn't have to tell her anything or ask her anything, but this is how cool she was. She would wait for my daddy to leave because coming over there while he was home . . . caused even more turmoil. And then she would just come over and take my mama grocery shopping. She'd take her to get groceries because she knew my dad didn't give her nothing for food. She would ask no questions, just take my mama shopping. . . . My mother kept a calendar, and every Friday when my father got paid she would write down how much he gave her. So, she knew how much she had to work with for the week."

Although Walter was feared at home and ignored by the churchgoing community, the street people loved him as someone who seemingly had no fear and who could make lots of friends. It is a description that fits his famous grandson.

In the larger society, black folks received a small measure of justice in 1954.

The *Brown v. Board of Education* decision prompted blacks in Norfolk to once more challenge the city's Jim Crow school policies. Central to their frustration were the tactics of U.S. Senator Harry F. Byrd who, in 1954, controlled Virginia state politics.

A Southern Democrat and segregationist, Byrd became a proponent of the "Southern Manifesto," written in 1956 by pro-segregation legislators who'd been angered by the Supreme Court's *Brown v. Board* decision. The Manifesto eventually carried the signatures of nineteen senators and eighty-one members of the House of Representatives, including the entire congressional delegations of the states of Alabama, Arkansas, Georgia, Louisiana, Mississippi, and South Carolina. The signers of the Manifesto wanted to ensure that the status quo racial hierarchy, i.e., whites in charge and blacks subservient, was maintained in perpetuity.

Senator Byrd meant to fight integration until the bitter end. On May 9, 1957, at the Banquet of the Hampton Roads Maritime Association of Norfolk, Virginia, he said:

> Let me be frank, we southerners are fighting this thing [integration] with our backs to the wall but what we lack in numbers we make up in our determination and will protect our Southern states and the welfare of our people.

Senator Byrd's remarks left little doubt that the black citizens in the state of Virginia were not included amongst those he considered to be "our people." But African Americans were not deterred. As Senator Byrd and his supporters worked to ensure the status quo, several black families in Norfolk filed suit against the city's school board for its failure to desegregate public schools. The original lawsuit had been filed in 1956, but three years transpired before any progress was seen.

While blacks struggled publicly for educational justice, at home the beatings became too much for Rosa Belle. Tupac's mother remembered the end of her parents' marriage: "One time in front of me and Glo my dad tried to hit her, and because we were there, my mother did not let that happen. We never saw that blow connect 'cause she threw hot grease on him. Right from the skillet she was holding. She never would have done that if she were alone with him." Rosa Belle finally left Walter, took her two girls back to Lumberton, and later moved to New York City.

The move helped eleven-year-old Alice escape the South's racial virulence. But taking refuge in New York City did not mean the end of social difficulties. Blacks in the North found that, aside from the methods and degrees of racism, they were still regarded as second-class citizens.

African Americans were frequently steered into undesirable areas near manufacturing industries. Municipal leaders felt no compulsion to invest tax dollars into paving roads, erecting street lamps, or laying sewage systems in outlying areas that were de facto designated for blacks.

The new frontier of life in the North, while not characterized by the racial virulence of southern bigots, was far from being a land of harmony and tolerance. In this environment, the survival skills that Alice learned in the South served her well.

Rosa Belle, Gloria, and Alice settled in the Bronx. It was a tough environment and by fifteen, Alice was running with a girl gang called the

Disciple Debs. They committed acts of vandalism, drank wine, and beat up strangers for fun.

But Alice had talent and passed the rigorous admissions process required by the High School of Performing Arts. Rosa Belle could not afford to buy Alice lunch or things like special leotards and other dance gear so Alice started cutting classes.

By the time she was eighteen, Alice and her thirty-three-year-old boyfriend, Ray, were getting high together on LSD and listening to the music of Sly Stone and Jimi Hendrix. In 1966 Alice left school. She was nineteen years old and spent much of her time partying and hanging out with her best friend, Sandra, who liked using heroin. Alice tried it once, got sick, and never used it again.

When Sandra died from a brain hemorrhage, Alice was devastated. She ended her relationship with Ray and started going to *bembes*, a drum ceremony that originated in the Yoruba culture of West Africa. Intrigued, Alice decided to study the religion and culture of the Yoruba people. She eventually took a new name, Afeni, meaning "dear one" and "lover of people."

This season of tumult in Afeni's life produced an intersection of people and events that permanently changed things for her. One person who affected Afeni and many other young blacks was Bobby Seale, Black Panther Party cofounder. When he visited Harlem in 1968, Afeni was in a huge crowd that gathered on 125th Street and Seventh Avenue to hear him speak. He talked about the Black Panther Party for Self-Defense, explained its program, and then announced that the party was opening an office in New York City.

four

THE BLACK PANTHER
PARTY FOR SELF-DEFENSE

President Lyndon B. Johnson's signing of the 1964 Civil Rights Act and the 1965 Voting Rights Act was testimony to the years African Americans spent fighting to win their basic constitutional rights. But those measures were, after all, mere laws that could be broken.

Political and economic power remained in the hands of the privileged few. As the glowing embers of the 1960s civil rights movement cooled, African Americans still labored against old miseries that had persisted from the moment in 1619 when twenty Africans had been ushered into lives of bondage at Jamestown, Virginia. The legacy of those conditions defined the world Tupac Amaru Shakur was born into. Its foundation rested on the hopes and dreams of people who had stretched American society beyond its established limits in the previous two decades in their search for political and socioeconomic justice.

The nation's military involvement in Vietnam, ostensibly to thwart the spread of communism, had stalled into a costly, grinding war of attrition that appeared to have no coherent strategy to pursue and no end in sight. The confusion produced by the failing effort in Vietnam was compounded by swelling opposition to the war at home. The struggle on the home front turned many of America's college campuses into zones of confusion and conflict. The May 4, 1970, murder of student protestors by the Ohio National Guard at Kent State University in Kent, Ohio, emphasized the degree to which civil order had disintegrated.

Giving the lie to American rhetoric about being a bulwark of freedom in the cold war struggle against Soviet and Chinese communism was America's hypocritical denial of first-class citizenship to millions of black Americans at home. By the early 1950s, after centuries of delay of these rights and freedoms, and continuation of violence, blacks decided that they'd had enough.

The civil rights movement that became a social revolution was energized by young people who believed in the philosophy of confrontational nonviolence espoused by Dr. Martin Luther King Jr., a youthful minister from Atlanta, Georgia. King and his followers pricked America's tortured conscience into reforming its ways.

But others had grown tired of chipping away at the hatred. These advocates for action insisted that racist fire be met with flaming indignation and, if necessary, armed resistance. Both the proponents of confrontational nonviolence and those advocating more vigorous action were shaken on April 4, 1968, when an assassin's bullet killed Dr. King as he stood on the balcony outside his room at the Lorraine Hotel in Memphis, Tennessee. King's murder underscored the rabid determination of northern bigots and southern segregationists to oppose the changes that could ultimately deliver full citizenship for African Americans.

"History is the long and tragic story of the fact that privileged groups seldom give up their privileges voluntarily," King had famously written from a Birmingham, Alabama, jail cell on April 16, 1963. "We know through painful experience that freedom is never voluntarily given by the oppressor; it must be demanded."

Just a few years earlier, in August 1955, fourteen-year-old Emmett Till, a Chicagoan visiting his cousins in Money, Mississippi, was brutally slain for allegedly speaking to a young white woman. The senselessness of Till's murder and the startling acquittal of his murderers—implicated by eyewitness testimony—proved to be a horrific reminder for blacks that the courts could not be depended upon to champion their cause. Power brokers who insisted that blacks quietly suffer through were just as willing to bend and break the law to achieve their aims.

The modern civil rights movement that began symbolically with *Brown vs. Board of Education* and gained traction with the rise of Rev. Dr. Martin Luther King Jr., coincided with the 1955–1956 Montgomery Bus Boycott. The warriors for justice were met with resistance at every turn. It was often violent, occasionally overwhelming, and always risked the possibility of terrorist retaliation. But some had moved beyond fear of intimidation.

In 1948, a former street thug and hustler named Detroit Red began a seven-year cycle of being shuttled through the Massachusetts state prison system. He used his time to read, ponder, think, and debate. He devoured books that stimulated his formidable intelligence. He studied and learned the history, processes, and philosophies that had crushed the will of black people through physical enslavement and imprisonment.

As a self-confessed criminal, he had unwittingly assisted those who had chained his mind and caged his body. He renounced his criminal ways and took a new name: Malcolm X. The birth of his new identity introduced a powerful voice that spoke with riveting boldness about the dismal history and contemporary conditions of blacks in America.

Far too many blacks had been left "fat, happy, and deaf, dumb, and blinded" by the crumbs they received from "the white man's rich table," Malcolm thundered. He exhorted blacks to open their eyes and start thinking. Only after they finally realized how numb and depleted they'd been left from the long sojourn in America's racist nightmare would they would fully understand that "from the first landing of the first slave ship" that generations of blacks in America had been "living like sheep in a den of wolves."

The grisly record of lynching had left a bloody trail across America's history. Whenever and wherever blacks possessed ambition, expected dignified treatment, or resented insult, mayhem soon followed. Whenever and wherever blacks were accused of a crime, whether real or imagined, torture and death at the hands of mobs was their doom. Whenever and wherever blacks challenged their suppression, bombings, murder, and pillaging was the frequent punishing response.

Years later, northerner and Harvard law professor Derrick Bell, recalling his first trip through the Jim Crow South, noted that the "trip . . . was traumatic. . . . My life and well-being lay totally at the whim of any white person I encountered. . . . The choice of courtesy or rudeness was theirs to make, mine to accept—or face the consequences."

The 1964 Civil Rights Act and 1965 Voting Rights Act were grand gestures and necessary steps to ensure that civil rights goals were achieved. But America had been down the path of signed documents and public ceremonies before. Always, the process of translating the spirit and language of those documents into reality lagged.

In 1964, the endless cycle of delayed action produced the black power movement. Originating in the ranks of the Student Nonviolence Coordinating Committee (SNCC, pronounced "snick"), this organization was initially in philosophical accord with Dr. King and the Southern Christian Leadership Conference (SCLC).

But society's intransigence thwarted the quest for civil rights, causing young blacks to seek more aggressive means to resolve grievances. They were unwilling to live the tortured lives of their parents whose quiet courage had nurtured and protected them from Jim Crow.

For a time, the most effective exponent of black power was Stokely Carmichael, a Trinidad native and Howard University graduate living in New York City. In 1966 he assumed the chairmanship of SNCC and shifted the organization's focus toward black nationalism and away from interracial collaboration. This redirection of purpose was characterized by more strident language and tactics than those used by Dr. King and his disciples of nonviolence. This new approach heralded the creation of the Black Panther Party (BPP), founded by Huey P. Newton and Bobby Seale in October 1966.

From the moment Newton and Seale established the Panthers they made it clear that they had no interest in pacifist integration and co-operation with the establishment. They meant to forcefully resist the establishment that had been the source of injustices perpetrated against blacks. They also sought to direct their efforts at the simmering anger of northern blacks who admired the actions of Dr. King and the SCLC but nevertheless languished under the hardships of urban racism.

By 1966—over one hundred years after the January 1, 1863, Emancipation Proclamation ending slavery; the April 9, 1865, ending of the Civil War; and the brief spurt from 1865 to 1877 when America had truly pursued liberty for all by outlawing slavery with the Thirteenth Amendment, strengthening civil rights through the Fourteenth Amendment, and extending voting privileges with the Fifteenth Amendment—blacks were still in bondage.

"We must face the tragic fact that the Negro is still not free," Dr. King lamented on the steps of the Lincoln Memorial on August 28, 1963. The lives of blacks were "still sadly crippled by the manacles of segregation and the chains of discrimination," as they tried to survive "on a lonely island of poverty in the midst of a vast ocean of material prosperity." By the middle of the twentieth century, blacks were "still languishing in the corners of American society" and living in exile within their own land.

For Huey P. Newton those extra hundred years had been more than enough. He was born in Monroe, Louisiana, on February 17, 1942, the youngest of seven children. When Huey was three, his family moved to Oakland, California, where his father, Walter, a Baptist minister, found work as a handyman and longshoreman. America's involvement in World War II created a demand for war materiel and labor, leading the Newton family to join thousands of other blacks who went west to find work.

Wartime necessities and the priority to defeat Nazi Germany and imperial Japan reduced domestic racial hostilities, but that changed with victory. Returning white soldiers forced blacks out of their jobs as society forced blacks into areas like Oakland where they were restricted to their neighborhoods. Harassment and intimidation by local law enforcement kept them confined.

The boldness that Huey Newton exhibited with the Black Panthers came honestly from the personality of his father. Walter Newton's reputation for strength and forthrightness in his family stemmed from the knowledge that he had dared to speak his mind to whites in Louisiana and had occasionally defied them as well. He prized loyalty to family, friends, and oneself. He believed in the power of God and the sanctity of the human spirit. For Huey and his six siblings, Walter Newton was not only a stern disciplinarian but a man of deep conviction and honor. He was their hero.

But family discipline and religious doctrine were not enough to prevent young Huey from venturing into the streets. Nor were they enough to mold him into a model student. He was largely illiterate until age sixteen as he was constantly facing school expulsion due to his penchant for fighting. Black Panther cofounder Bobby Seale later observed that Huey's violent nature earned him the respect of pimps and gangsters who were familiar with his "toughness and badass character."

Growing up on the hard side of "Oak Town," Huey and other young blacks literally fought their way through life. Street combat was its own form of communication as young men jettisoned their frustrations and boredom, and asserted their identities. Those qualities coalesced in 1966 in the wake of the devastation caused by the Watts riots.

Trouble had been brewing for a long time in Watts, the center of the black community in Los Angeles. By 1965, the citizens of Watts had weathered years of overcrowding and unemployment, suffered the ravages of crime and drug addiction, and had difficulty accessing adequate health care facilities and public transportation.

Those circumstances were worsened by the brutality of the Los Angeles police force. The frustration boiled over on August 11, 1965, when a white police officer pulled over a black motorist on suspicion of drunk driving. A crowd gathered. Police reinforcements were called. Tempers flared. Soon there was a riot.

For the next week, trouble stalked the city. By the time it was over, thirty-four were dead, nine hundred injured, more than four thousand arrested, leaving $35 million in property damage. The crisis that engulfed Watts was indicative of the dangerous tensions in many northern cities where, like their southern counterparts, generations of urban blacks had tried to succeed along the social margins. As in the case of Watts, the police supplied a frequent source of antagonism.

The violence of the Watts riots not only illustrated the participants' desperation but signaled their refusal to passively suffer the ills of heavy-handed law enforcement. The Community Alert Patrol was formed, consisting of members from a variety of activist organizations. Armed with cameras, law books, and tape recorders, CAP observers kept an eye on police activities in black communities.

The Black Panther Party offered Afeni an opportunity to put her street skills and intelligence to use for tangible change. For her the Black

Panthers were simultaneously a way out, a way up, and a way to answer black people's crisis of identity in America.

Early on, BPP founder Huey Newton declared, "We're gonna defend ourselves." Echoing the determination of slain leader Malcolm X, Newton vowed that that defense would be conducted "by any means necessary."

It soon became apparent that, in addition to vigorously answering the violence visited upon blacks, they also intended to change the fundamental nature of the nation's social systems. The new world the Panthers hoped to achieve was articulated in the October 1966 Black Panther Party platform and program entitled "What We Want, What We Believe."

This list of ten points reflected the frustrations of the time while illustrating, with some degree of poignancy, the extremes to which the Panthers felt that they (and black people) had been pushed to gain basic human rights in the United States:

1. *We want freedom. We want power to determine the destiny of our Black Community.* We believe that black people will not be free until we are able to determine our destiny.

2. *We want full employment for our people.* We believe that the federal government is responsible and obligated to give every man employment on a guaranteed income. We believe that if the white American businessman will not give full employment, then the means of production should be taken from the businessman and placed in the community so that the people of the community can organize and employ all of its people and give a high standard of living.

3. *We want an end to the robbery by the white man of our Black Community.* We believe that this racist government has robbed us and now we are demanding the overdue debt of forty acres and two mules. Forty acres and two mules was promised 100 years ago as restitution for slave labor and mass murder of black

people. We will accept the payment in currency which will be distributed to our many communities. The Germans are now aiding the Jews in Israel for the genocide of the Jewish people. The Germans murdered six million Jews. The American racist has taken part in the slaughter of over fifty million black people; therefore, we feel that this is a modest demand that we make.

4. *We want decent housing, fit for shelter of human beings.* We believe that if the white landlords will not give decent housing to our black community, then the housing and the land should be made into cooperatives so that our community, with government aid, can build and make decent housing for its people.

5. *We want education for our people that exposes the true nature of this decadent American society. We want education that teaches us our true history and our role in present day society.* We believe in an educational system that will give to our people a knowledge of self. If a man does not have knowledge of himself and his position in society and the world, then he has little chance to relate to anything else.

6. *We want all black men to be exempt from military service.* We believe that Black people should not be forced to fight in the military service to defend a racist government that does not protect us. We will not fight and kill other people of color in the world who, like black people, are being victimized by the white racist government of America. We will protect ourselves from the force and violence of the racist police and the racist military, by whatever means necessary.

7. *We want an immediate end to POLICE BRUTALITY and MURDER of black people.* We believe we can end police brutality in our black community by organizing black self-defense groups that are dedicated to defending our black community from racist police oppression and brutality. The Second Amendment to the Constitution of the United States gives a right to bear arms. We therefore believe that all black people should arm themselves for self-defense.

8. *We want freedom for all black men held in federal, state,*
   county, and city prisons and jails. We believe that all black
   people should be released from the many jails and prisons
   because they have not received a fair and impartial trial.

9. *We want all black people when brought to trial to be tried in court by a jury*
   of their peer group or people from their black communities, as defined by
   the Constitution of the United States. We believe that the courts should
   follow the United States Constitution so that black people will receive
   fair trials. The 14th Amendment of the U.S. Constitution gives a man
   a right to be tried by his peer group. A peer is a person from a similar
   economic, social, religious, geographical, environmental, historical,
   and racial background. To do this the court will be forced to select a
   jury from the black community from which the black defendant came.
   We have been, and are being tried by all-white juries that have no
   understanding of the 'average reason man' of the black community.

10. *We want land, bread, housing, education, clothing, justice and peace.*
    And as our major political objective, a United Nations supervised
    plebiscite to be held throughout the black colony in which only the
    black colonial subjects will be allowed to participate for the purpose
    of determining the will of black people as to their national destiny.

In later years, Afeni commented that "the way he said those ten points
made me want that more than anything. So there I was wrapped in my
Africanness. . . . There was now something I could do with all this ag-
gression, and all this fear" because "up until this point, I wasn't shit. . . .
Robbing people, beating up people. That wasn't shit. Before I joined
the party, I was fucked up. I would slap a motherfucker in a minute. I
cussed my mama out, disrespected her, left her cryin' on the kitchen
floor. Would you be proud of that shit? I left home and lived with any
brother off the street that would pay my way. . . . I'd cut somebody just

for the hell of it and never look back. They [The Panthers] educated my mind and gave me direction."

The Panthers fully intended their ten points to be more than the ramblings of disaffected social revolutionaries. They backed up their statements by creating an organization that was multifaceted, far-reaching, and structured so that it left no area of the United States untouched. Each party chapter was organized by state, and within "a chapter were branches, organized by city, and within branches were sections," and those "were divided into subsections which were divided into squads."

The Panthers' paramilitary structure with its chain of command and communications networks, their broad acceptance and espousal of a Marxist ideology that made capitalism the culprit of black oppression, and their belief in the lowest classes of blacks (the lumpen proletariat), which included "millions of . . . domestics and porters, nurse's aides and maintenance men, laundresses and cooks, sharecroppers . . . ghetto dwellers, welfare mothers, and street hustlers," made the Panthers unique, dynamic, and, to the establishment, dangerous.

The Panthers' leadership reminded itself that the anger of lower-class blacks during riots in the early part of the twentieth century shook society to its core. By the mid-1960s, this population still existed on the outer fringes of America's material wealth and sociopolitical benefits.

Lower-class blacks, even more than those in the middle class who suffered discrimination but not the same degree of economic despair, represented a mass that the Panthers strove to "educate and politicize . . . creating vanguard soldiers from the hard core . . . of black people ready for revolution."

The Panthers forced their way into the public consciousness in May 1967 when they challenged an attempt by the state of California to outlaw their right to carry weapons during neighborhood safety patrols. Malcolm X's frequent exhortations for black people to defend themselves against violence, including violence caused by the police, was the foundation from which the Panthers justified their actions for community self-defense.

The legislation was sponsored by Donald Mulford, a wealthy state assemblyman who, from Huey Newton's perspective, intended to "suppress the people's constitutional right to bear arms." Newton charged that "until then, white men had owned and carried guns with impunity." He added that the "bill was further evidence of this country's vicious double standards against Blacks."

Years of wrangling with a system that "beat down poor and oppressed people" led Panther leaders to conclude that they would not win their fight against the gun bill. They fought back anyway and took their concerns to the state legislature in Sacramento. With the many reporters and photographers who were certain to be present, this tactic provided the most effective means of spreading the message in Executive Mandate Number One prepared by Huey Newton:

> The Black Panther Party for Self-Defense calls upon the American people in general, and Black people in particular, to take careful note of the racist California Legislature now considering legislation aimed at keeping Black people disarmed and powerless while racist police agencies throughout the country intensify the terror, brutality, murder, and repression of Black people. . . . Black people have begged, prayed, petitioned, demonstrated and everything else to get the racist power structure of America to right the wrongs which have historically been perpetrated against Black people. All of these efforts have been answered by more repression, deceit, and hypocrisy. . . . The Black Panther Party for Self-Defense believes that the time has come for Black people to arm themselves against this terror before it is too late. . . . A people who have suffered so much for so long at

the hands of a racist society, must draw the line somewhere. We believe that the Black communities of America must rise up as one man to halt the progression of a trend that leads inevitably to their total destruction.

With the statement ready, Newton directed Bobby Seale to expose to the world the legislature's attempt to deprive black citizens of their right to bear arms. Seale arrived with a small contingent of thirty Panthers, armed and wearing their distinctive black leather jackets and black berets.

Photographs of the event spread around the world, elevating the Panthers' profile and attracting new recruits into chapters being established across the nation. They also put themselves directly in the gaze of the U.S. government.

The ideological climate of the cold war had kept American leaders poised to counteract threats to national security. By the 1960s, the FBI applied the lessons it had learned from keeping watch over social movements to leaders and members of the civil rights movement through a process of surveillance known as the Counterintelligence Program (COINTELPRO). Established in 1956, its purpose was to "police radicals" in the United States.

The emergence of charismatic, determined national black leaders who meant to eradicate northern racist and southern segregationist strangleholds on black life posed direct challenges to establishment power structures. FBI director J. Edgar Hoover was determined to nullify the people and organizations that were the sources of those challenges.

In August 1967, he ordered COINTELPRO to focus its attention on black nationalist movements for the purpose of causing internal dissension, neutralizing their effectiveness, and ultimately destroying their power as avenues of discontent. In 1969, Hoover described the Panthers as the "greatest threat to the internal security of the country," due to their "Marxist-Leninist ideology" and their numerous alleged "assaults on police officers."

The Panthers had "engaged in violent confrontations with police throughout the country," Hoover asserted, noting that Panther leaders had traveled "extensively all over the United States preaching their gospel of hate and violence not only to ghetto residents, but to students in colleges, universities and high schools as well."

The FBI's efforts to sow discord within the ranks of the Panthers took a variety of forms:

- **Eavesdropping:** a massive program of surveillance via wiretaps, surreptitious entries and burglaries, electronic devices, live "tails" and mail tampering.
- **Bogus mail:** fabricated correspondence between members of targeted groups or between groups to foster splits within or between organizations.
- **Black propaganda operations:** the fabrication and distribution of publications (leaflets, broadsides, etc.) attributed to targeted organizations and/or individuals designed to misrepresent their positions, goals, or objectives in a way that publicly discredited them and caused group tensions.
- **Harassment arrests:** the repeated arrest of targeted individuals and organization members on spurious charges not with any hope of real convictions but to simply harass, increase paranoia, tie up activists in a series of prearraignment incarcerations and preliminary courtroom procedures, and deplete their resources through posting of numerous bail bonds.
- **Infiltrators and agents provocateurs:** the infiltration of targeted organizations by informers and agents provocateurs, the latter expressly for the purpose of fomenting or engaging

in illegal activities which could then be attributed to key organizational members and/or the organization as a whole.

- **Pseudo gangs:** organizations designed to "con-
fuse, divide, and undermine" as well as do outright battle with authentic dissident groups.
- **Bad-jacketing:** the practice of creating suspicion by
spreading rumors, manufacturing evidence, and so on,
that bona fide organizational members, usually in key
position, are FBI or police informers, guilty of such of-
fenses as skimming organizational funds and the like.
- **Fabrication of evidence:** fabricating evidence for criminal prosecution of key individuals and withholding of exculpatory evidence that might serve to block conviction of these individuals.
- **Assassination:** the outright physical elimination of se-
lected political leaders, either for "exemplary" reasons or after other attempts at destroying their effectiveness failed.

As the FBI probed deeper into the Panther organization, its leadership continued resisting suppressive policing agencies. "The real danger comes from highly organized establishment forces," Huey Newton
commented. It was those elements who were "dangerous and who come
into our communities every day to commit violence against us, knowing that the laws will protect them."

But changes and crises in the Panther leadership caused discord in
the ranks and forced it to scale back the public persona of a group prepared to wage armed struggle. COINTELPRO proved effective and
eventually caused the public to turn against the Panthers.

It did not help matters that Huey Newton, who had been imprisoned
in 1968 for murder but was eventually acquitted, was again charged with
murder and assault in 1974. Tensions with other pro-black organizations
like Ron Karenga's United Slaves (Us) also poisoned relations.

On January 17, 1969, events turned violent on the UCLA campus when Panthers Alprentice "Bunchy" Carter and John Huggins were murdered in a shootout with supporters of Us for allegedly making derogatory remarks about Karenga.

While the Panthers on the West Coast struggled against government attempts to destroy them, Panthers on the East Coast fought to maintain their vision. The proud and defiant Black Panthers changed the perspective of black men that Afeni had developed. After hearing Bobby Seale speak in 1968, Afeni accepted his challenge to join the Panthers.

Afeni became a section leader. This opportunity for Afeni to lend her energy to the movement occurred just as local undercover police officers from New York's Bureau of Special Services (BOSS) were infiltrating the organization.

Afeni started a free breakfast program for children, gave speeches, did fund-raising, and worked harder than she ever had for black freedom. She even found personal happiness in a romantic relationship with a Panther named Lumumba, who was one of the Harlem leaders.

Lumumba Abdul Shakur was born Anthony Coston on January 9, 1943, in Atlantic City, New Jersey. He converted to Islam while he was in prison and changed his name. By the time Afeni met him, he was married (according to Islamic law) to a woman named Sayeeda and had two children.

Since Islamic law allowed him to have more than one wife, he married Afeni in 1968. She was twenty-one years old. Their bliss was short-lived.

On April 2, 1969, she and twenty-one other Panthers were arrested and charged with conspiring to "murder New York City policemen and dynamite five midtown department stores, a police precinct, six railroad rights of way, and the New York Botanical Gardens."

From the point of view of renowned French novelist and playwright, Jean Genet, the only crime committed by the New York 21 and the larger Panthers organization had been their boldness in daring to defy the establishment. "From the day, the moment, I was arrested from my sleeping bed on 117th Street, the fight was on," Afeni later noted. "From April 2, 1969, until May 13, 1971, I fought for everything I believed in, against everyone I knew, not only the government but my own Panther brethren . . . and even Lumumba."

Afeni and her codefendants were each charged with thirty counts of conspiracy. She faced 351 years of incarceration if convicted on all counts. Bail was set at $100,000, and it took months for liberal white celebrities, including Leonard Bernstein and Jane Fonda, to gather the money to free her. She was released pending trial on January 30, 1970.

While out on bail, Afeni was seeing two men: a Panther named Billy Garland and Kenneth Saunders, a gangster who went by the name of Legs, who had once worked for the infamous drug lord Nicky Barnes. She got pregnant by Billy and a hurt Lumumba (who had not raised bail and was still incarcerated) promptly divorced her for adultery.

After enjoying months of freedom on bail, she was thrown back into prison when several of her codefendants jumped bail.

She said, "I got pregnant while I was out on bail. . . . I never thought that I wasn't going to spend the rest of my life in jail. I was never getting out and that's why I wanted to have this baby. . . . Because I wanted to leave something here. . . . If I thought I was getting out, I never would have had the baby. I probably would have gotten an abortion."

The trial lasted nine months even though the prosecution didn't have a strong case. Afeni represented herself. While grilling their chief witness, she forced him to admit that he had never seen her commit an illegal act.

The jury took only two and a half hours to return a not guilty verdict. She was released a month before she gave birth on June 16, 1971, to her first child, a boy she named Lesane Parish Crooks. As godfather she named Geronimo Pratt, a high-ranking Black Panther Party official who had been jailed the year before on charges of murdering a twenty-seven-year-old schoolteacher during a botched robbery. A young Johnnie Cochran was part of his defense team and, despite evidence that indicated Pratt was nowhere near the scene of the crime, he was sent to prison for the next twenty-seven years. The godmother was Assata Shakur (no relation), also a Black Panther Party member. When her godson was six years old, she was convicted of murdering a New Jersey State trooper and escaped from prison in 1979 to live in Cuba under the protection of Fidel Castro.

More than thirty years later, Afeni reflected on her time in the Black Panther Party: "We lost it. We dropped the ball. We didn't know what we were dealing with. We were in over our heads. And, worst of all, we were not listening. We were not listening to old people. We had removed any semblance of spirituality from our movement. . . . Not having a spiritual base, not acknowledging the greatness of God, not saying we can't do this without God, we had no solid ground. Instead, we turned against God, and how you gonna win like that?"

five

LESANE GETS A NAME CHANGE

Beating a life sentence in prison did not quell Afeni's revolutionary sentiments. Less than two years after her release, she changed her son's name from Lesane Parish Crooks to Tupac Amaru Shakur. The inspiration came from history.

Tupac Amaru (1571–1572) was last emperor of the Inca people and the fourth son of another Incan emperor, Manco Capac, who ruled from 1533 to 1545. Tupac Amaru's exploits as a ruler who resisted Spanish colonial domination and social injustice has earned him a contemporary following, especially in Latin America.

Among the Quechua people in the sixteenth century, the word "Inca" meant "prince" or "king" and also applied to each supreme ruler of the empire and generally to all of the empire's subject people. In 1533, when the Spanish conquered Cuzco and the Incan empire, they sought to maintain the appearance of an indigenous monarchy as a means of governing Peru. Manco Capac was crowned as the Inca in that year and carried out his duties for two years. In the second year, he led a rebellion against the Spanish that ultimately failed. Nevertheless, Manco's desire for independence remained strong and he established the community of Vilcabamba approximately thirty miles northwest of Cuzco.

When Manco died in 1545, his empire at Vilcabamba was ruled by each of his four sons in succession. By 1571, Tupac Amaru, the fourth of Manco's sons, had ascended to the throne in the same period when the new Spanish viceroy of Peru, Francisco de Toledo, had determined that it was time to bring an end to the Incan empire at Vilcabamba.

In 1572, Spanish soldiers aided by Native American allies captured Vilcabamba along with Tupac and his followers. Tupac was subsequently brought to Cuzco where he was tried and sentenced to death. On November 14, 1572, Tupac Amaru was decapitated in the central plaza of Cuzco in front of thousands of Spanish and Native American onlookers. After the execution, Toledo ruled over the Incan people with great brutality.

The indigenous people suffered from European illnesses (smallpox, measles, and influenza) to which they had no immunity. Thousands were conscripted (i.e., enslaved) to work in the silver mines. In 1780 José Gabriel Condorcanqui, also known as Tupac Amaru II, led the first major Incan uprising against the Spaniards in two centuries.

For all of his bravery, though, Tupac Amaru II fared no better than his namesake. The rebellion was suppressed and he was captured and sentenced to death. In 1781 Tupac Amaru II was tortured, and then he was drawn and quartered on the main plaza in Cuzco and decapitated.

Giving her son a name associated with such a bloody legacy should have given Afeni pause. But the name was also a symbol of resistance, and that was important to her. Unfortunately, her son was not a warrior by nature. He was a sensitive soul who preferred to daydream and write poetry. In time, he would try to remake himself into a badass—and the results would be disastrous.

part two
SURVIVOR

six

WHO PLANS A
MOTHERLESS CHILD?

*A*feni gave birth to her son thinking that her sister, Gloria, would raise the child. Although Afeni came up with this plan under extremely arduous circumstances, it still reeked of narcissism. By the time Tupac was born Gloria was married to a man named Thomas Cox and had children of her own. Afeni's reasoning indicates a high level of self-centeredness. Who was she to change her sister's life so drastically?

Tupac later told a reporter, "I was cultivated in prison, my embryo was in prison." Tupac astutely concluded that his period in utero had quite possibly produced some side effects that he carried through life.

Dr. Sonja Trent-Brown, assistant professor of psychology at Hope College in Holland, Michigan, has noted that:

> Maternal stress during the prenatal period can produce negative developmental outcomes in the developing embryo and/ or fetus. In fact, maternal stress is referred to as a teratogen,

which is a harmful substance, experience, or agent that can adversely affect prenatal development. The level and timing of the stress would be the key aspects to consider, and the stress likely experienced with respect to incarceration would be great, certainly more than sufficient to produce deleterious effects. The timing of the teratogen exposure is usually the most harmful during the embryonic phase, followed by the fetal phase. In this case, Afeni was incarcerated for 8 months, which would span both the embryonic and fetal periods. The negative developmental outcomes due to extreme maternal stress could include cleft lip/cleft palate, sex differentiation, low birth weight, spontaneous abortion, emotional problems, and behavior disorders. It is important to keep in mind that mothers who experience stress during pregnancy are also likely to continue to experience stress after the baby is born, which creates an environment which could contribute to increased risks for cognitive, psychosocial, emotional and behavioral outcomes for the infant.

It was a harsh beginning for Tupac, but because Afeni's life was so chaotic during his early years, things got much worse. The Black Panther Party was dying but it still had active groups that held meetings and rallies. Afeni often attended, carrying Tupac with her.

Family friend (and later Tupac's publicist) Karen Lee has said, "I met him for the first time at the Armory in New York City on 168th Street. I had gone over to hear Minister Louis Farrakhan speak at a rally and Afeni was there with him. He was a tiny baby about two months old."

Afeni was a free woman, but as an unskilled high school dropout she had a hard time finding work. That difficulty was compounded by her being an ex-Panther once accused of conspiracy to bomb New York landmarks. Immediately following her release, Afeni accepted invitations to speak at colleges and universities (including Harvard). When black radicalism stopped being chic among the white upper classes, Afeni's audiences vanished and so did her income.

As Tupac grew he was taken to more protests and rallies. Some events started in the afternoon and continued late into the night until someone carried him to wherever home was for that night. At best it was an apartment that Afeni had rented. Sometimes it was a homeless shelter. Other times it was a relative's sofa. The term "black power" was "like a lullaby when I was a kid," he later said.

Afeni eventually found employment at a nonprofit organization that provided free legal services to the poor. By the time Tupac started kindergarten, Afeni had married a man named Mutulu Shakur (no relation to her first husband) and had another child, a girl she named Sekyiwa.

Jeral Wayne Williams (a.k.a. Mutulu Shakur) was born on August 8, 1950, in Baltimore, Maryland. In the 1970s, Mutulu had been a prominent figure in an experimental detox program at the Lincoln Hospital in the South Bronx. He helped heroin addicts try to kick their habit through acupuncture. In 1978, New York Assemblyman Charles Schumer complained to the *New York Times* that Lincoln Detox was riddled with problems relative to financial accountability and mismanagement. Mayor Ed Koch soon placed the program under hospital management and had staffers connected with Shakur reassigned.

Tupac was ten when his stepfather, Mutulu, became a fugitive from justice. It was around this time that a minister asked the boy what he wanted to be when he grew up. "A revolutionary," he replied.

By the late 1970s, America had grown weary of the social upheavals of the 1960s. But for some of the "revolutionaries" who'd protested everything from racial inequality to the Vietnam War, there was more work to be done.

The establishment that had been the focus of so much ire remained intact. This was the perspective of Mutulu Shakur and followers who joined him in a new venture: the Black Acupuncture Advisory Association of North America (BAAANA).

The group moved into a Harlem brownstone and focused on providing health care that was free from NYC control. Joining Mutulu were remnants of the Weathermen, a 1960s radical group that advocated change through armed struggle.

The Weathermen, also known as the Weather Underground, were their own brand of trouble. The group had formed in 1968 in response to the failure of the antiwar and civil rights movements to fully and effectively end the war, eliminate racism, and implement a vast range of reforms for social justice. Their name was taken from Bob Dylan's "Subterranean Homesick Blues": "You don't need a weatherman to know which way the wind blows."

The Weather Underground bombed targets across the United States through the 1970s, selecting places they deemed emblematic of strife and violence around the world. They wanted to get the attention of the authorities and had accomplished that objective earlier in the decade when a group of them accidentally blew up three of their members along with a townhouse on 11th Street in New York's Greenwich Village.

They had been attempting to construct an antipersonnel mine such as the kind the United States used in Vietnam. They wanted Americans to experience directly the horror of such a weapon. With the plan literally backfiring, the Weather Underground became the object of an intensive fugitive hunt.

By the late 1970s, a sad few of the Weather Underground remained. These last true believers joined similarly splintered remnants of the New Black Panthers Party, the Black Liberation Army, and the Republic of New Afrika. In 1978, the disgruntled but still zealous members of the various organizations formed into a group known as the Family.

According to government prosecutors, Mutulu and the Family began robbing banks and then armored cars. By the summer of 1980, they had amassed more than $900,000. The cash was supposedly going to be used to finance a revolution. The perpetrators intended to transform the states of Mississippi, Louisiana, Alabama, Georgia, and South Carolina into a territory inhabited only by black people. Notably absent were details regarding how the latest generation of the descendants of slaveholders, Klansmen, segregationists, and plain old everyday people would be removed from the land.

The group's grandiose dream of establishing a southern black republic was interrupted on October 20, 1981, with the robbery of a Brinks truck in Nyack, New York. The robbery left three dead, including security guard Peter Paige and Nyack police officers Waverly Brown and Edward O'Grady.

Famed radical Kathy Boudin was arrested at the scene, but Mutulu Shakur escaped with the FBI in full pursuit.

Afeni got fired from her job, most likely because her employer was troubled by her association with Mutulu. She and her two children were left to shuttle back and forth between relatives' homes and shelters. Tupac recalled that they moved from Manhattan to the Bronx and back at least eighteen times from the time he was born until he was ten years old. Tupac said that each time "I had to reinvent myself. People think just because you born in the ghetto, you gonna fit in. A little twist in your life and you don't fit in, no matter what. I felt like my life could be destroyed at any moment."

Such a lifestyle had profound effects on young Tupac, risking equally profound consequences. "I was crying all the time," Tupac later told an interviewer. "My major thing was I couldn't fit in, because I was from everywhere. I didn't have no buddies that I grew up with." Dr. Sonja Trent-Brown notes that, "The lack of stability may be one of the most damaging experiences a child can have."

Human development is characterized not only by change over the lifespan, but also by consistency and coherence. In order to most effectively develop skills—cognitively, emotionally, socially, even bio-socially—children need consistent experiences. During toddlerhood children attune to the patterns of events and activities in their lives. They find comfort in the consistency of their daily routines. When there is a lack of consistency, children are left with no structure within which to interpret their lives. They become insecure and uncertain, and live life never knowing what might happen next.

As a child, Tupac learned to cook and sew. He said, "When I was young, I was quiet, withdrawn, I read a lot. I wrote poetry. I kept a diary."

Poetry skills were not particularly valued in his family, among his mother's compatriots, and certainly not in the tough ghetto neighborhoods where he lived. It frustrated him that he "didn't feel hard" like the folks around him.

Tupac's next "daddy" was a gangster who once worked for infamous drug dealer Nicky Barnes. Afeni's new boyfriend went by the name of Legs, and Tupac became very attached to him.

It was Legs who introduced Afeni to crack cocaine. "That was our way of socializing," she recollected. "He would come home and stick a pipe in my mouth."

Young Tupac, who loved poetry and writing short stories, was ill-equipped to compete in a world filled with drugs and gangsters. The difficulties posed by those challenges were likely compounded by a conflicting range of sentiments.

The strong link between African American mothers and their sons had long been recognized in the black community. The connection provided the foundation for the assertion that black mothers often "loved their sons but raised their daughters."

The love African American mothers showered on their sons emanated not only from the natural processes of maternal function but the desire to protect their sons from the devastation awaiting black boys as they matured into manhood. The perceived necessity to protect has often been reinforced by the tragic absence, or intermittent presence, of black fathers in the lives of their children.

Black boys, filled with all of the natural and social predispositions to fulfill their roles as "man of the house," could be caught in a conflicted world of submitting to their mother while also feeling charged to protect and provide for her. This was the position that Tupac found himself in as he grew.

Being too young to provide for and protect Afeni and Sekyiwa didn't mean that Tupac missed the social signals communicating those activities as being the responsibilities of men. Confronting his mother's multiple boyfriends, who purported to provide some modicum of relief in those areas, couldn't detract from an innate recognition that they were ultimately no good for her or him.

He was too young to challenge or understand the presence of such men in his mother's life. Whatever relief or inspiration they brought for the moment was not enough to trump the devastation and chaos that usually followed in their wake. Worse, his cousins teased him about his features (the long lashes, high cheekbones) and about the fact that he couldn't play ball or fight very well. Of his New York boyhood, Tupac once lamented, "I didn't feel hard."

Given the circumstances, Tupac learned to hide his true feelings. A cousin sensed that Tupac needed help and told Afeni about free acting classes in Harlem. Twelve-year-old Tupac enrolled and was chosen for the role of Travis in a community production of Lorraine Hansberry's *A Raisin in the Sun*. Tupac loved it: "My first acting job was at the Apollo Theater when Jesse Jackson was running for president. It was a fundraiser. . . . when the curtain went up, I just caught that bug."

Sekyiwa recalls, "We were absolutely homeless, no place to go during the daytime. And if he took this part with this theater ensemble on 125th Street playing Travis in *A Raisin in the Sun* at the Apollo, then he and I would be able to be inside of a building for a period of time and we would have food and so what acting and theater did to us is that it fed us. It fed us for a period of time when he was twelve and I was nine."

In the meantime, Mutulu was still on the run but sometimes snuck back into the neighborhood to see the children. He would not approach or speak to them. He simply smiled and waved at them from a distance. It was his way of letting them know that he hadn't forgotten them and still cared about them. He has said "When I would feel he needed me, I'd do whatever I had to, to get there even if it was just so that he could see me—and he'd wave, so happy."

Since Mutulu was on the FBI's Ten Most Wanted list, Tupac was often approached by government agents about contact with the fugitive. Torn by his affection for his stepfather and intimidated by the law, Tupac lied and said that he had not seen Mutulu. It was all very confusing for the young boy.

The family's situation worsened when Legs went to jail for credit card fraud. Unable to pay the rent once again, Afeni, Tupac, and Sekyiwa moved in with Gloria and her family. Then Afeni packed up her children and left New York City for good. Their next stop was Baltimore, Maryland.

seven

NONVIOLENCE IS A DEAD
PHILOSOPHY

The difficulties Tupac Shakur experienced as a child—maternal drug abuse, social isolation, federal agents, fugitives, and deeply flawed father figures—occurred within the larger context of social apathy and decay. By 1971, the year of Tupac's birth, the United States was already hurrying past the halcyon days of the civil rights movement when the progressive dreams of millions seemed finally within grasp. Much of that retreat had begun on April 4, 1968, when Dr. Martin Luther King Jr. was assassinated.

Several years earlier in 1963, author James Baldwin had caustically observed that "there is no reason that black men should be expected to be more patient, more forbearing, and more farseeing than whites.... The real reason that nonviolence is considered to be a virtue in Negroes ... is that white men do not want their lives, their self-image, or their property threatened." The murder of Dr. King, the "last prince of nonviolence," opened floodgates of anger that put major sectors of society at risk as cities around the country erupted into chaos.

"Nonviolence is a dead philosophy," lamented Floyd McKissick, national director of the Congress of Racial Equality (CORE). Black power advocate Stokely Carmichael warned that the "rebellions that have been occurring around these cities is light stuff to what is about to happen. We have to retaliate for the deaths of our leaders."

The year of King's death also witnessed the election of Richard M. Nixon, who had already made a name for himself as a staunch cold warrior. Nixon structured his 1968 presidential campaign to appeal to America's "silent majority," those beleaguered Americans who'd not only grown weary of civil rights demonstrators but had felt increasingly threatened as blacks gained greater access to education and opportunity. From their vantage point, the rapid changes taking place across the country had disrupted the establishment and many sought leadership that would restore law, order, and stability.

The loss of King also coincided with the slow crumbling of the Great Society envisioned by President Lyndon B. Johnson (1963–1968). A New Deal Democrat who deeply admired Franklin Delano Roosevelt, Johnson had invested much of his domestic political capital into a war on poverty.

"The Great Society rests on abundance and liberty for all," Johnson proclaimed in a commencement address at the University of Michigan in May 1964. "It demands an end to poverty and racial injustice to which we are totally committed in our time." With those words Johnson announced his intention to end the disgrace of economic disparity in America and finally achieve the social and racial justice that had languished beneath the heel of Jim Crow segregation.

Johnson used the powers of the presidency to create popular programs like Head Start (to help disadvantaged preschoolers), Upward Bound (aimed at bolstering the skills of impoverished teens who wanted to attend college), and Medicare (which provides medical assistance for the elderly). While the war on poverty was designed to benefit all, it was unique in that many of its initiatives (e.g., the New Careers Program) involved poor African Americans who took an active role in their design and implementation.

But President Johnson's crusade against poverty fell victim to the war in Vietnam. The president also faced stiff opposition from southern politicians who worried that their influence was being undercut as the once voiceless and socially disenfranchised gained more power. Friction had also developed between Johnson and King over the latter's increasing condemnation of U.S. policies in Vietnam.

By the end of 1968, an election year, King was dead and Johnson, severely weakened from devastating reversals in Vietnam, announced his retirement from politics. The new president, Richard M. Nixon, an establishment iron horse, won over his domestic supporters by presenting a more stern resolve to the demanding civil rights, antiwar factions that had shaken the nation.

But in the paradoxical fashion that soon defined his presidency, Nixon also implemented a number of affirmative action programs to "stifle black militancy." Over time, those programs served as a safety valve for channeling "festering black resentment."

But Nixon's enlightenment had its limitations. In an attempt to further widen a growing rupture between civil rights workers and white union members, Nixon made sure that a Johnson initiative, the Philadelphia Plan, was enforced. This program required that "minority workers in the notoriously discriminatory construction trades be hired in rough proportion to their percentage in the local labor force." Nixon hoped that in disgusted response to such federal intervention, white union members would align themselves and their votes with the Republican Party.

eight

THE NEW START

Afeni, Tupac, and Sekyiwa moved to Baltimore in 1984, and at first they stayed with Walter's sister Sharon. At only thirteen and ten years of age, it was impossible for the youngsters to understand their mother's inner pain and confusion. She was separated from her sister, lacking job skills, and sad because so many of her former comrades were dead or in jail. Nevertheless, Afeni tried to make a good life for herself and her children. She got on welfare, signed up for free computer classes, and spent her free time making sure that the kids were doing well in school. By all accounts, they were happy for the first two years—but it was a tough town.

Baltimore city officials and citizens were battling the plague of crack cocaine. But the major news was the Baltimore Colts' move to Indianapolis, Indiana. The poverty, crime, unemployment, and the desperation of the underclass was sad competition against headlines concerning the machinations of super wealthy sports team owners and their rich athletes.

The closure of the Bethlehem Shipyard in 1983 was part of an ongoing industrial and economic realignment across the nation. The resulting unemployment increased the stresses on poor and working families. The decay of America's urban centers had also been accelerated by riots in the aftermath of Dr. King's assassination. Like vast sections of Detroit after the 1967 riots, the Hough section of Cleveland, Ohio, in 1966, Baltimore by 1984 was working to restore its infrastructure and image.

White flight had been under way for some years before the riots; in the aftermath, weary home and business owners succumbed to despair and left the city for good. The problems they left behind hastened the spread of drugs, the violence associated with drugs, and draconian governmental economic policies.

Shortly after they arrived from New York, Afeni learned that Legs, although released from jail, had died from a crack-induced heart attack. "That hurt Tupac," Afeni remembered. "It was three months before he cried. After he did, he told me, 'I miss my daddy.'" She enrolled Tupac in the Roland Park Middle School and his old friend, Darrin Bastfield recalled Tupac's impoverished appearance in his book *Back in the Day*:

> On his [Tupac's] first day in mid-November he walked into homeroom late.... He wore baggy pants of thin blue fabric, like surgical scrubs, with staples encircling the bottom of each leg along the hem. The pants hung loosely from his skinny frame, below a generic long-sleeve shirt tucked in at the waist where a drawstring held the rag-tag ensemble in place. His hair was lopsided, like some two-tiered wannabe Bobby Brown cut. And he exposed poorly kept unfinished braces along both rows of teeth with every parting of his lips. Only the metal anchors were in place on each tooth; no wires connected them.

He was an object of ridicule for the two years he attended Roland Park, but he never complained. Sekyiwa says, "We lived in Baltimore for four years. The first two years were the happiest for me. We had weekends over my Aunt Sharon's. We had things to do. Nothing political. We had noodles, and it was fun. It was regular people's life."

But times got hard again. For reasons that are not clear, Afeni had trouble paying the electric bill and the family lived in darkness. "We didn't have any lights," Tupac said.

> I used to sit outside by the street lights and read the *Autobiography of Malcolm X*. And it made it so real to me, that I didn't have any lights on at home and I was sitting outside on the benches reading this book. And it changed me, it moved me. And then of course my mother had books by people like Patrice Lumumba and Stokely Carmichael, *Seize the Time* by Bobby Seale and *Soledad Brother* by George Jackson. And she would tell these stories of things that she had done or seen and it made me feel a part of something. She always raised me to think I was the Black Prince of the revolution.

The situation at Tupac's house was otherworldly. Darrin Bastfield recalled that Tupac's

> skinny apartment stretched down the length of the front door hallway to a closed door at the end, with a couple rooms branching off to the right. The rooms were not conventional rooms, just space broken up into areas to be used differently at different times. The largest room at the front of the apartment functioned as the living room, while the next room down the hallway was both the dining room and a sleeping area. Tupac introduced me to his younger sister, Sekyiwa, in what was the living room. . . .

At the end of the hall we stepped into a small dark room that seemed to me a pantry, where Ms. Shakur lay resting on the well broken-in mattress of a small single bed. . . . Before we sank any further into small talk, Ms. Shakur produced ten dollars and told Tupac to run out and fetch her a sack. This shocked and bewildered me, but I said nothing.

The following year, 1985, Tupac started attending Paul Lawrence Dunbar High School. His fortunes changed for the better when he auditioned for the Baltimore School for the Arts and landed a spot at the much sought after institution. He said, "The high school I went to was mostly for white kids and rich minorities."

A drama major, Tupac found himself immersed in a strong academic program and a broad range of arts instruction, which included voice and ballet.

In February 1986, Mutulu's life on the run came to an abrupt end as he was tackled by police on a Los Angeles street corner, thrown to the ground, and arrested. He was tried, convicted, and sentenced to sixty years in prison.

nine

BALTIMORE SCHOOL
FOR THE ARTS

Tupac's attending the Baltimore School for the Arts harnessed his creative talent, gave him an outlet for its expression, and focused his desires for the future. In 1980, the school had a total enrollment of only sixty-eight students (by the early twenty-first century that number nearly quadrupled).

The idea for the school originated within the school district in 1977. The goal was to found a school for students who wanted to pursue a career in the arts. This intentional distinction underscored the far-reaching nature of what the Baltimore school board sought to accomplish.

Students generally attended the school closest to them. Magnet schools offered specialized curriculums and programs; a side benefit (sometimes theoretical) of the magnet system was the diverse student population. The original desire of the school board to establish an institution like the BSA resulted in the creation of a task force to study the school's proposed administrative and academic structure, including course offerings. The task force consisted of employees from the school district and representatives from the arts and business communities. As the task force did its work, Mayor Williaam Donald Schaefer obtained federal money to renovate an old hotel into a school. The work went forward and with the establishment of a board of overseers and the granting of a 501(c) (3) status, the district gave the BSA its charter.

Being an institution that offered something special like a magnet school but was even more unique in its curriculum design and academic focus from "regular," "magnet," and other "charter" schools underscored just how different the BSA was when it was established. With a daily schedule that allowed for four periods of academics and four periods of instruction in a student's chosen major, the BSA allowed students to develop and hone their creative skills while enriching their minds.

Further enhancing the success of the school was its charter and its ability to remain relatively autonomous. A particularly nice feature for students from Baltimore was the free tuition. This undoubtedly brought a measure of relief to Tupac since his resources from home were severely limited and unpredictable.

ten

THE BAKKE DECISION

Many of the difficulties Tupac faced in Baltimore were like those of other poor Americans—they were beyond his ability to control or influence. Many of the people associated with those issues were government policymakers whose faraway actions in the halls of power often materialized as tangible hardships in the lives of the disadvantaged.

The political cataclysm caused by the Watergate scandal during Richard Nixon's second term distracted lawmakers for months as they unraveled the web of intrigue. Revelations that Nixon had been directly tied to the five men who'd burglarized the Democratic National Headquarters at the Watergate Hotel in Washington, D.C., in June 1972 stunned the nation.

In subsequent investigations, Americans were treated to a burlesque of corruption and rogue criminality that extended from the White House into the private sector and beyond. The tumult associated with the civil rights movement paled in comparison to the blows sustained by the body politic from Watergate.

President Nixon resigned on August 8, 1974, and was succeeded by Vice President Gerald R. Ford, who'd become vice president when Spiro T. Agnew had resigned in 1973. In April 1975, President Ford ordered all Americans still in Vietnam to leave the country.

After two decades, 58,000 dead, and billions spent, Vietnam was lost. Many of the dead were from the forgotten urban and rural zones of America. These powerless and voiceless citizens had borne the burden of the country's missteps in Indochina, returning home in shame and bitterness. The angst of the period was captured in popular culture.

Philip Caputo's *A Rumor of War* (1987) presented a riveting narration of the mindless ideology that had seized America during Vietnam and made the nation its prisoner. In 1978, James Webb, a Naval Academy graduate and Marine infantry officer (who went on to serve as assistant secretary of the Navy) wrote *Fields of Fire*. His gritty tale of Marines struggling to support each other, maintain their humanity and morale, and do their duty while despising the war, presented a searing indictment of civilian and military leadership.

John M. Del Vecchio's lamentation in *The Thirteenth Valley* (1982) confirmed that no part of a soldier's mind, body, or spirit survived unscathed by the horrors of Vietnam. Such artistic indictments against the war were no less impassioned on the big screen.

Michael Cimino's film *The Deer Hunter* (1978) explored the haunting experiences of three blue-collar Pittsburgh steelworkers whose lives were shattered by the brutality of Vietnam. Francis Ford Coppola's epic *Apocalypse Now* (1979) highlighted the insanity and wastefulness of the conflict. In 1986, Oliver Stone's *Platoon* presented a chilling exploration of Vietnam's ability to turn a civilian draftee into a killer. Stanley Kubrick's *Full Metal Jacket* (1987) offered a Faustian journey into Vietnam's surreal impossibilities. And in the 1995 film, *Dead Presidents*, African American codirectors, Albert and Alan Hughes, boldly demonstrated the ways in which black soldiers struggled against race and class in both Vietnam and America.

Many African Americans were striving to take advantage of the new-found opportunities offered by affirmative action when a 1978 Supreme Court ruling signaled a shift in the direction of the nation's civil rights agenda. That shift was the beginning of a reorientation of priorities that had profound effects on the lower class that Tupac was born into.

When a white Vietnam veteran named Alan Bakke had his application to the medical school at the University of California rejected, he sued the university. The dispute centered on the university's affirmative action practice of setting aside sixteen of the one hundred places in each entering class for disadvantaged minority students. In response to a 1976 ruling by the California Supreme Court that ruled in Bakke's favor, the University of California appealed to the U.S. Supreme Court, which subsequently followed suit.

As the *Bakke* decision loomed, blacks wondered about the long-term consequences of a ruling upholding the plaintiff's complaint. Whites, however, "lined up before the United States Supreme Court the night before the . . . case was to be argued" to "make certain . . . that sacred American racial principles would not be destroyed." In the end, the Court judged it more important to uphold those racial principles.

Before long the phrase "reverse discrimination" became a rallying cry for the opponents of affirmative action policies. They contended that preferential treatment and the establishment of quotas for individuals of historically disadvantaged groups was in itself discriminatory and violated the equal protections clause in the Fourteenth Amendment of the Constitution. There were also pernicious comparisons between groups that had worked themselves into America's socioeconomic mainstream without the use of such programs.

The simmering dissatisfaction of affirmative action's opponents soon erupted into outright hostility. And just as part of the civil rights movement had died on a Memphis hotel balcony with King, the vision of social justice that had inspired Lyndon Johnson's Great Society was corroded by a Supreme Court decision.

As the 1970s drew to a close, Americans retreated inward to reflect on events from the late 1950s, 1960s, and mid-1970s. The celebratory outpouring of bicentennial melodrama on July 4, 1976, was not enough to lift the nation from its malaise over the debacles of Vietnam and Watergate.

New York City stood as a grim example of the late 1970s collapse of hope and vision that had propelled so many to the heights of goodwill during the 1960s. Financial strains, employment dislocation, soaring poverty rates (especially in Brooklyn and the Bronx), de facto segregation, and inadequate education further darkened the horizon of opportunity for inner-city youth.

The cycles of individual destitution and community decay became more commonplace. Cities like St. Louis, Milwaukee, Cleveland, Detroit, and Newark were facing the challenges of urban segregation and declining socioeconomic fortunes. Overall, years before Tupac arrived in Baltimore, it and other cities across the nation were steadily losing ground in the battle to house, educate, and employ young people.

But youngsters like Tupac who came of age in the 1980s refused to be silent about social inequity. For the beleaguered children of New York City a favorite form of expressing their angst was graffiti. "The Big Apple's subway cars and stations became as much canvases as transportation," and anyone astute enough to "see beyond the nuisance caused to travelers" understood that graffiti was "the voice of kids using spray paint and Magic Markers to scream for attention."

The plight and protests of inner-city blacks and Latinos grew louder as the nation's economy, increasingly tied to the globalizing marketplace, became more unpredictable and less accessible for the poor.

By 1980, just a few years before Tupac's move to Baltimore, national patterns hinted that the new decade would be a rough one for blacks and Latinos. Falling wages, diminished opportunities for unskilled workers, and increasing income disparities between the wealthiest and poorest segments of society characterized their world. It was from such a world that the energy and creative genius of Tupac Shakur took flight.

It was during the Baltimore years that Tupac wrote his first rap, calling himself MC New York, and participated in high school rap competitions. Mining through the drama of his past, he drew his first rhymes from an incident involving the shooting of a friend. Word got around that he was a very skilled rapper, and he began to dream of someday landing a record deal and becoming recognized in the hip-hop community.

eleven

YEARS OF LEAN
AND PLENTY OF MEAN

𝕴t was no accident that America, during Tupac Shakur's teenage years, was more interested in maximizing its material wealth than addressing the plight of its most vulnerable and desperate citizens. In 1980, Republican presidential candidate Ronald Wilson Reagan, a former actor and governor of California (1966–1970; 1970–1974) defeated James Earl "Jimmy" Carter in his bid for reelection.

Reagan's victory ushered in an era known as the "Reagan revolution," exemplified by a new approach to governance that sought, in part, to boost the optimism of the American people through tax cuts while reducing their reliance on government. The "revolution" was a good thing for many, but it had little to offer inner-city children like nine-year-old Tupac Shakur.

In America of the 1980s, when Tupac Shakur transitioned from childhood into young adulthood, influential power brokers with access to inside financial information routinely cheated their way to staggering wealth. In the process, they sent shock waves of economic trauma into the lives of the nation's citizens.

The 1980s was the decade of the Wall Street inside trader, the financial business cheat, and unchecked corporate excess. Filmmaker Oliver Stone's 1987 movie *Wall Street* addressed the rampant problems in the business world's securities sector. In one of the film's most unforgettable scenes, actor Michael Douglas, playing the role of ruthless corporate raider Gordon Gekko (appropriately named after a lizard) made a speech to stockholders, highlighting the problems within the financial sector:

> I am not a destroyer of companies. I am a liberator of them! The point is, ladies and gentlemen, that greed—for lack of a better word—is good. Greed is right. Greed works. Greed clarifies, cuts through, and captures the essence of the evolutionary spirit. Greed in all of its forms—greed for life, for money, for love, knowledge—has marked the upward surge of mankind. And greed—you mark my words—will . . . save . . . that other malfunctioning corporation called the USA.

Few people exemplified the ethical blight of the business world's financial sector during the 1980s as well as Ivan Boesky and Michael Milken. Boesky, who is a graduate of the Detroit College of Law and whose father was a Russian immigrant who became a successful restaurant owner in Detroit, started his career on Wall Street in 1966 as a stock analyst. By the mid-1980s, "Ivan the Terrible" Boesky had amassed a fortune that was worth an estimated $200 million. The workaholic Boesky routinely put in twenty-hour days, conducting business as an arbitrageur at his Manhattan office where he traded in the stocks of companies that were likely targets for takeovers. While this was normally a legal activity as long as the trade was based on publicly held knowledge of an imminent acquisition, Boesky bent the rules to ensure his enrichment.

On November 14, 1986, the Securities and Exchange Commission charged Boesky with illegal stock manipulation based on insider information. Also known as "insider trading," this type of activity caused massive harm to companies and working people. As later defined by Thomas C. Newkirk, associate director of the SEC's Enforcement Division, the insider trading of the 1980s was best defined as activity that occurred "when those privileged with confidential information about important events" used that "special advantage . . . to reap profits or avoid losses on the stock market to the detriment of . . . typical investors who buy or sell their stock without" the advantage of similar information.

Several months earlier in May, while delivering the commencement address at the University of California's business school at Berkeley, Boesky told a cheering audience, "Greed is all right. . . . Greed is healthy. You can be greedy and still feel good about yourself."

This ethos was embraced by government policymakers who did their part to cast the working poor and destitute as lay-abouts and good-for-nothings whose inherent laziness was the source of their troubles. Conversely, the corruption and larceny committed by the coiffed and presumably cultured threw the nation into one convulsing crisis after another.

The good times ran out with Boesky's arrest. In exchange for leniency, he agreed to cooperate with the SEC and taped conversations he had with other inside traders, notably Michael Milken, a brilliant and tireless financial wizard at the firm of Drexel Burnham Lambert.

Eventually amassing a fortune estimated at $1 billion, Michael Milken was the undisputed king of junk bond trading. Despite the name, junk bonds were valuable IOUs from corporations that stated how much investors would be paid back on a future date, adding in interest that accrued on the borrowed money. Milken turned "junk" into gold as he operated out of his posh offices in Beverly Hills, making over four hundred calls per day as he built and maintained his empire. It came crashing down when the government, using information supplied by Boesky, charged Milken with insider trading.

The deeper SEC investigators looked into the matter the more ethical rot they found, and it was not long before Milken's firm, Drexel Burnham Lambert, was also feeling the wrath of federal law enforcement. For some who had entrusted Drexel to lend reputable advice in navigating the economic turmoil of the period, knowledge of the firm's malfeasance came too late.

For example, while the SEC gathered information to move on Boesky and eventually snag Milken, the world's largest rubber company, Goodyear Tire & Rubber in Akron, Ohio, waged a valiant fight to stave off a hostile takeover by Anglo-French corporate raider James Goldsmith. On October 29, 1986, chairman of the board Robert E. Mercer issued a memo to Goodyear employees, stating that the company had engaged the investment firm of Goldman Sachs & Co. and Drexel Burnham Lambert to provide assistance in "studying a possible restructuring of our assets and/or our capital structure."

In that same memo, Mercer noted that:

> Today the American economy and the nation's industry base is threatened by a flaw in our free enterprise system which enables outsiders to buy up this country's industrial base with its own assets. In all too many cases, to pay off the resulting indebtedness, the companies affected by a takeover are often broken up.

On November 4, 1986, Mercer went on to lament that the stock purchases Goldsmith and his associates had made "were carried on with a high degree of secrecy while taking full advantage of America's liberal laws which allow raiders to establish a significant position in a company's stock prior to any discussions with that company or any disclosure to the SEC."

Deficiencies in those same "liberal laws" combined with lax oversight and glacially paced enforcement also contributed to the problem. Thus it was small comfort to Goodyear employees when on April 14, 1990, Milken was sentenced to ten years in jail and fined $650 million. Boesky was eventually sentenced to three years in prison, fined $100 million, and banned for life from dealing in securities. Raider Goldsmith eventually died in 1997 from a heart attack subsequent to his four-year battle with pancreatic cancer. By the time of Goldsmith's death, Goodyear Tire & Rubber had been dismembered and was on its way to losing market share as it struggled to recover from the raid and keep pace with increasing global competition.

For Tupac Shakur's struggling family, the combination of troubles resulting from Wall Street malfeasance and governmental policies heaped more burdens onto people in their category. Social Security disability benefits were diminished. Unemployment grew. The number of Americans without medical insurance expanded. Free school lunch programs were eliminated. The tax system was repeatedly manipulated to favor the rich while imposing greater burdens on the working class. And, as usual, the general impoverishment affecting so many was felt most often and hardest by Latinos and African Americans.

The results of societal attitudes that supported or at least acquiesced to governmental policies that punished the poor so that those who had much could get more were incalculable. Reagan era advocacy of a "trickle down" economic theory hinged on the belief that as the position of the wealthiest Americans improved, their good fortune would be magically manifested in the lives of the middle classes and the poor.

Rising unemployment rates, deterioration in the inner cities, and a significantly diminished commitment to defending civil rights should have demolished that fiction. But those who were leading the assault on the most vulnerable elements in American society enthusiastically moved forward with their agenda.

twelve

JADA AND JOHN

Tupac met two people who would become his lifelong friends: Jada Pinkett and a white guy name John Cole. He would later immortalize both friends in one of his many poems, which have all been published in a collection entitled *The Rose That Grew From Concrete*.

Tupac once admitted that before entering the Baltimore School of the Arts, he believed that white people were "devils" who hated him simply because he was black. Donald Hicken, his drama teacher, says, "I don't think Tupac had been around white people that much before he came to this school. I think he had a fairly implanted chip on his shoulder about white people. And I think that what he learned here was that when you take away the power structure element of white culture, and you get down to the grassroots level of white culture, it's very easy to relate across the races." As it turned out, the high school had a predominately wealthy, mostly white student body, and to his surprise, he was accepted into their ranks and made lots of friends. As Tupac gained exposure to alternate social realities, he learned the value of maintaining an open mind.

Tupac was happy at school because he did not have to pretend a toughness that he did not feel. He was intellectually curious, excelled in his classes, and entered school talent competitions where he rapped using the stage name MC New York. At home, though, things were still tough.

Sekyiwa has spoken about this time period: "Other times . . . we were homeless and my mom would get a job but we would have no place to go while she was at work. She would take us to the movie theater back when you could pay one price and just stay there all day and we would watch *Krush Groove, Beat Street,* and *Breakin* over and over again until it was time for mommy to get off work."

Regarding the precariousness of Tupac's home life, Dr. Sonja Trent-Brown has observed that:

> His [Tupac's] mother's addiction would compound feelings of social isolation and rejection due to her unavailability—both emotionally and as a provider. He would likely be placed in the position of having to be the primary provider and caregiver for his sister and his mother, providing for them by whatever means he was able, regardless of social appropriateness or legality.

Tupac told a close friend that his mom was a former Panther, and a local activist named Truxom contacted him. They spoke of how drugs had not only destroyed the black community but allegedly had been distributed to specific communities to hasten gentrification through the forced dislocation of residents.

Truxom accepted this conspiracy theory, believing that institutional elements intended to destabilize areas with people of color, wait until property values dropped, and then utilize law enforcement to depopulate. After that, with land cheap and no one collectively opposing the effort, once blighted areas would be turned into posh communities for the wealthy and well-connected.

Truxom's Yo-No campaign against guns appealed to Tupac and his white girlfriend, Mary Baldridge, a student in the high school's dance department. She was an attractive young woman who'd been brought up to look past color and see people as people.

Tupac and Mary worked together on the Yo-No campaign, going from door to door, telling residents about the issues and inviting them to meetings. They wrote a short operetta to dramatize that problem and teen pregnancy, taking their message and their passion to churches and schools around town, winning the support of just about everyone who saw their production of six players. Displaying early signs of his musical future, Tupac wrote raps for organizational rallies that sometimes included collaborations with groups like the NAACP.

Throughout the Yo-No campaign, Tupac won converts by speaking forthrightly of his own experiences and imploring his audience to take his message seriously. This public activity in combination with the nurturing environment of the Baltimore School for the Arts did wonders for his confidence and dignity, which had been eroded by life in the ghetto.

Tupac also made friends with an ex-student named John Cole who'd been in the visual art department. Jada Pinkett had introduced them and they became good friends. Tupac and Jada became lifelong friends, showing a special care and concern for each other that lasted until the end of Tupac's days.

Jada Koren Pinkett was born on September 18, 1971, in Baltimore, Maryland. Her parents, Adrienne Banfield and Robson Pinkett Jr., married after her mother, still in high school, discovered she was pregnant. The marriage didn't last.

Along with her striking good looks and determination to succeed, Jada's personality more than matched that of the vibrant Tupac. They were both strong-willed and direct in their way of dealing with people, and shared a close kinship. "We were a lot alike in a lot of ways," recalled the future wife of actor Will Smith. "We both had mothers who were using at the time, and that was a real difficult struggle for us both."

Jada noted that those shared difficulties brought out "a lot of insecurities on both of our parts." He was poor, she explained. "I mean, when I met Tupac, and this is not an exaggeration, he owned two pairs of pants and two sweaters. Okay? He slept on a mattress with no sheets when I went into his room, and it took me a long time to get into his house because he was embarrassed. He didn't know where his meals were coming from." Tupac liked Jada, but circumstances and people seemed to prevent them from forging a romantic bond.

At home, life had become chaotic once more and Tupac bore the burden of being a teenage "man of the house." He experienced relief and freedom at John's. He spent as much time in John's Bolton Hill, upper-middle-class neighborhood as possible. There he found a sense of refuge and relaxation.

Tupac had fun over at John's, with people streaming through all of the time. Food, liquor, and marijuana were always in good supply, and there were clothes and other amenities like sheets for beds that most people took for granted. For Tupac, John's world was like falling into a gold mine. John's parents, far from being resentful about Tupac mooching off of their son, shrugged him off and satisfied themselves with being happy if their son was happy.

Beneath it all, however, there were troubles in John's world. Like Tupac, John hadn't known his biological father. His mother was struggling with her health.

However, John exposed Tupac to new ways of living, laughing, and interacting with other people. Tupac was amazed by the size of John's room, which was a loft overlooking the living room. It had great space and plenty of high-class comforts.

Tupac gladly accepted his friend's largesse, which extended to wearing John's clothes, and he was happy to be away from home. Even John's previously worn clothes were better than what Tupac had. Tupac was a focused competitor. His childhood hadn't left much room for second chances. He existed in a world that didn't suffer fools and operated according to the harsh rules of survival.

BSA was the right place for Tupac. His experiences there did more to build his self-esteem and creativity than he could've gotten elsewhere in the city. The creative curriculum and the artistic freedom allowed the students to grow in their special ways, expressing themselves without inhibition, and basically nurtured them into adulthood. All of this in addition to John's home provided Tupac with an alternate universe into which he could gladly escape.

Eventually John moved in with his older brother in Reservoir Hill, just under a mile away. It wasn't as nice as John's family home, but was good enough, and Tupac didn't hesitate to join him, since it was still far better than living at home.

Tupac didn't take up much space in the two-bedroom apartment. He and John slept on different couches while John's brother and a friend named Richard took the two bedrooms.

As before, John and Tupac spent much time discussing everything from political systems to metaphysics. Their bond was strengthened by John's dating Jada. Tupac was satisfied to see two good friends of his happy with each other.

Moreover, being with John and other white friends relieved Tupac of his responsibility to champion the downtrodden. Being with them, he could simply be a young guy, growing into manhood and having fun.

And then it was over. Tupac arrived home at the Reservoir Hill complex one day and was told that he'd have to move out. John's brother was moving into another building, and there'd be no room for him.

Tupac, stunned, tried to fathom how his close friend could do such a thing to him. But from John's perspective, Tupac had been using him as a crutch and he was no longer willing to serve that purpose. A series of letters from Tupac to John didn't change the situation but rather irritated John since Tupac was being so dramatic. Tupac was desperate.

Going home was out of the question. In the end, Tupac stayed on in the apartment with Richard.

Richard was older and focused on the grim moneymaking realities of life. He was not enamored with having a drifting high school student living with him. The difficulties usually worsened when it was time for Tupac to come up with his portion of the rent.

But still, they enjoyed each other's company. Whether the two of them were discussing LL Cool J, Peter Gabriel, Sun Ra, Jimi Hendrix, or Eric Clapton, Tupac knew the artists, their life stories, and their music. It was not hard to be amazed by the depth and breadth of his knowledge. But it was amazing to witness, especially since his own background suggested nothing that would have made him so conversant on so many different subjects.

Those were good times. One teacher of Shakespeare, Richard Pilcher, recalled that Tupac "could have done a pretty good Hamlet."

But life never stayed good too long for Tupac. In the middle of his junior year, after he had completed his college applications, Afeni found out that they were being evicted. She decided to leave the state and start over yet again. Since Tupac was underage, he could not stay on at Richard's house without her consent. Tupac and Sekyiwa would have to leave Baltimore and go stay with an old political comrade of hers in Marin City, California. Having to leave BSA devastated Tupac and changed the course of his life. When he climbed on the bus that would take him to the West Coast, he carried five dollars in his pocket and four chicken wings in a paper bag.

Afeni's problems were common to ex-revolutionaries of all races. Many experienced chronic joblessness, homelessness, and drug addiction. Huey Newton himself eventually died of gunshot wounds received during a reputed drug deal gone bad.

Donald Hickens, who was also Tupac's mentor, recollected that the young thespian-rapper showed up in his office distraught about the news that he had to leave the school: "He was just heartbroken."

thirteen

THE JUNGLE

Tupac and Sekyiwa arrived in Marin City, across the bay from Oakland, in 1988. He was seventeen years old and she was thirteen.

They went to the home of Assante, a woman Afeni had been close to during her Black Panther days. Assante lived in a poor housing complex that was rife with crime. In fact Marin City's crime rate had soared to such levels that people referred to the community as "the Jungle."

The boy who arrived in "the Jungle" was a deep-thinking bohemian who understood the works of Shakespeare and had donned a leotard for his dance classes and acted in several school plays. He was not a street tough. Sekyiwa was a smart, sweet girl who longed for stability. The kids were in way over their heads.

Assante had agreed to house them, so Afeni sent the kids ahead of her until she could come up with some money for a ticket of her own. One day she got a call from Assante saying that the kids needed a new home.

When Afeni got to Marin City, Assante was nowhere to be found. Tupac and Sekyiwa were with a neighbor. Afeni had no idea what her kids had been enduring. Assante was a raging alcoholic who often passed

71

out on the floor and lay there sleeping for hours. She didn't cook regular meals and never lost an opportunity to let them know that their presence was a burden.

Assante, the onetime revolutionary, had shriveled into a mean drunk who habitually cursed them out. She saved most of her venom for Tupac, who represented every black male who'd ever hurt her or let her down.

Afeni had to find a new home for them fast but she had no money. While waiting for a government-subsidized apartment, the kids were farmed out to locals.

Tupac was the neighborhood underdog. "Niggas that wasn't shit and I knew it used to dis me . . . I got love but the kind of love you would give a dog or a neighborhood crack fiend."

Matters worsened when Afeni started using drugs again. Rapper Manny Man remembered that Tupac "stayed with us for a little while because his sister was dating my brother." And that wasn't all that Tupac was doing. "I was broke, nowhere to stay. I smoked weed. I hung out with the drug dealers, pimps, and the criminals. They were the only people that cared about me at that point. My mom, she was lost at that particular moment. She wasn't caring about herself. She was addicted to crack. It was hard, because she was my hero. I didn't have enough credits to graduate. I dropped out. I said I gotta get paid, I gotta find a way to make a living. I started selling drugs for like two weeks and the drug dealer said give me my drugs back, cuz I didn't know how to do it."

The dealer who'd been Tupac's boss was no pillar of the community, but he at least knew his business well enough to tell his former employee to leave the drug game alone. Tupac had shown a talent for rapping and that was where he needed to put his energies.

Tupac missed the curriculum at his old school. Tamalpais High School in Marin City was no haven for a boy who had recently been studying creative arts. He earned money as a pizza delivery boy and tried to pretend not to care about books and formal education. "I didn't fit in," Tupac later stated. "I was the outsider. . . . I dressed like a hippy, they teased me all the time. I couldn't play basketball, I didn't know who basketball players were. . . . I was the target for street gangs. They used to jump me. . . . I thought I was weird because I was writing poetry and I hated myself, I used to keep it a secret. I was really a nerd."

Tupac had few options and had even failed as a marijuana dealer. That proved to be a positive development, however, since it kept him out of harm's way. In the meantime, he rapped whenever he could and wherever someone would listen. Tupac crashed in different places while Afeni searched for a place for them to live. She found an apartment and kept on using cocaine.

He gained a reputation as someone who couldn't play basketball but was truly stunning on the microphone. By the time he met a white music promoter named Leila Steinberg, she had already heard of him.

fourteen

LEILA

Leila Steinberg was a rare ray of refreshing light and good luck that entered Tupac's life right when he needed her most. Tupac adjusted to life on the West Coast more quickly due to Leila's interest in him. His first steps on the road to fame and superstardom were made possible by her good connections and her big heart.

Growing up amid the activist atmosphere of the West Coast fostered Leila Steinberg's eventual involvement in programs, community action, and organizations dedicated to social justice and social reform. As the daughter of a criminal defense attorney, she had frequently witnessed the strange workings of the justice system. Those observations had demonstrated that system's inherent prejudice against the poor and the disenfranchised.

Leila also witnessed the human tragedies that frequently resulted from the bureaucracy's preoccupation with processing cases rather than rendering merciful justice. Those methods raised the likelihood that troubled, disadvantaged youths would become social problems. But still, what moved this white woman to devote so much time and energy to Tupac Shakur when he was just another pair of eyes staring out from a sea of black faces?

Leila's background supplied the answer. She was born in 1960 in Los Angeles, grew up in Watts, and attended black schools. She acquired the second sight that allowed her to see the truths of society's posture on education and culture concerning black people and others of color. Growing up in Watts during the 1970s as one of the few white kids in the area, she learned that her color was an advantage. Black kids used her to plead with school administrators for things that they needed because the powers that be would listen to Leila. She also realized early on that her white skin meant that she could get away with just about anything in an inner-city school. Leila's Mexican-born mother, who had roots in the Middle East, encouraged Leila to participate in acts of social protest, mostly for the rights of migrant farmworkers. Her restless mother left Leila with her father to pursue her crusades full-time, and Leila fell under the influence of her grandfather, who introduced her to a broad range of salsa, Brazilian, and Latin dances. In time, she started performing and learned West African dances along the way.

Her life was a whirlwind after high school. She researched music and artists and enrolled in college in Panama. Then she resided in northern California where she took college courses and toured with Congolese and Latin artists. She next went on the road with Carlos Santana's band and the R&B soul group the Neville Brothers. Then she married Bruce Crawford, an African American who was deeply involved with the L.A. rap scene, and they had a daughter.

Leila was intrigued by rap. It was fresh. It was honest. It captured her attention in a way that wouldn't let go. Life quickly got interesting. Bruce was gathering fame as a DJ and moved the family to the Bay Area and eventually farther north as his fame grew.

Although the West Coast was more progressive than other parts of the country, blacks were not welcomed into mainstream society, especially in California. Racism and prejudice had flowed south, north, and west in previous decades. By the late twentieth century, even in the aftermath of *Brown v. Board*, prejudice was still a battle being fought across the nation. As a result, Bruce sometimes "faced difficulties renting facilities to hold rap concerts and club parties," so he and Leila started promoting shows that sometimes drew up to 10,000 kids to a single event.

Leila got involved with the schools to ensure that her kids were getting a good cultural and academic education. Before long she was working with the nonprofit educational agency Young Imaginations, which was dedicated to bringing artists into the local schools to entertain students. Leila helped reorganize the agency into a "multicultural arts and education agency that used artists from a variety of races, ethnicities, and cultures to help educate ... children about history, culture, and politics."

Leila began addressing high school assemblies during the day while helping Bruce promote rap shows at night. The power of rap continued to impress her with its potential to speak to young people, and their enthusiastic responses to it confirmed her suspicions. So Leila founded her own organization.

Leila's lifetime exposure to various cultures, languages, and ideas had prepared her well. She directed her efforts into the schools of Marin City and Oakland, hoping to affect students in ways that made a positive difference in their lives. The passionate sincerity she brought to the free after-school workshops on writing and performance helped spread the word about her program, and she was soon teaching hundreds of students.

Meanwhile, an associate of Leila's, Lawanda Hunter, repeatedly told her about a new and promising talent. "I found somebody in Marin who just moved here," Hunter explained, adding that he was "everything you're looking for [in a person] to collaborate with." Leila acknowledged the news but paid little attention, especially since such leads had become commonplace.

Several weeks rolled by. Leila and Bruce did a promotional party at an area club. As Bruce attended to his DJ duties, Leila danced on the floor and soon found herself moving with "this very beautiful young person." She helped Bruce finish up and called it a night.

The next day Leila had an early afternoon workshop in Marin City but decided to stop by the park and read *A Part of My Soul Went with Him* by Winnie Mandela. She was sitting on the grass reading when a young, male voice said. "Give me a break. What do you know about Winnie Mandela?" Leila turned and saw the "beautiful young person" she'd danced with the night before.

It is highly unlikely that this meeting was an accident, although Leila believed it was. Tupac and every other aspiring rapper in the Bay Area knew that she held weekly auditions. Dozens of young artists usually descended on the space trying to win a chance to showcase their talent. Everyone knew that she had connections in the music industry. If you were part of the underground Bay Area hip-hop scene and wanted to hit the big time, you had to impress the white girl of hip-hop. If you wanted a record deal, Leila was a person to get to know. Rather than wait for a chance meeting or lining up outside her audition spaces, the charming and enterprising Tupac probably sought her out.

They reintroduced themselves, laughed, and celebrated the good fortune of finally meeting. A conversation quickly ensued and Leila soon understood that she had someone special in her presence.

Leila took Tupac to that evening's tryouts. He impressed her and everyone else he met that night. She invited Tupac to her class; he accepted. He was impressed with her teaching and passion but had ideas on how she could be more effective. Tupac soon became the focal point of her professional life and, a few months later, the two of them founded

Assemblies in Motion (AIM), an organization that brought talented performers to high schools in the area. "He changed who I am as a woman and as a parent," Leila later observed. "As Pac entered our group, he took a lot of my infantile thought processes to the next level."

In time, Tupac shared with Leila his chaotic home life. She realized that Afeni was "so addicted that his house was too dysfunctional to have a career or to keep going to school." Soon Tupac moved in with Leila and her family.

Leila discovered that, for all of his energy, drive, and talent, Tupac Shakur was a slob. He preferred to buy new clothes rather than wash the ones he had. Getting him to clean up after himself was a losing battle. But even so, he was a captivating presence. "At 17, he was wide-eyed and really believed that he could change the world."

For Tupac, changing the world meant preparing the mind, so he read through the books in Leila's library. No subject was off-limits. His interest scaled the intellectual heights of history, philosophy, politics, Eastern thought, culture, anthropology, and more.

This wasn't passive reading; he often challenged the authors' premises and conclusions, questioning their cultural biases and motivations. He also founded a rap group called Strictly Dope that performed at many local shows to great acclaim.

Leila worked to help launch Tupac's career by reaching out to Atron Gregory, manager of a popular rap group called Digital Underground. "I had talked with Atron, and I wanted to get us [Leila and Tupac] a deal," Leila recalled later. "And he [Atron] said that we had to make a video. We decided to have our own here [in the neighborhood] on the grass so that we could show Atron how tight we were. And so all of the kids in the building [Leila's apartment building] were our audience right here on the grass. . . . And we had a Strictly Dope show."

The show was a success and Atron Gregory was very impressed by the videotape.

Tupac was on the way to becoming a star. When he left Leila's home, he entrusted her with all of his important papers and dozens of poems, which she gave to Afeni after his death.

"We are all indebted to Leila, Tupac's first manager and adult friend, for her integrity in looking after the safety of his work," Afeni once said.

Leila Steinberg deserves a lot more credit than that. She nurtured Tupac by becoming the mother he needed. She gave him a safe place to stay and wholesome food to eat. She read great literature with him and the two discussed world issues and big ideas. She "argued with him about his ideas and career direction. She supported him through his personal and career crises. After he became famous, she listened to his boyish pride in his famous conquests. . . . She provided unflagging love to an artist she saw rapidly transform from a sweet-faced teen to an internationally recognized superstar."

fifteen

SHOCK G

Atron urged Digital Underground's leader, Gregory E. "Shock G" Jacobs, to meet with Tupac. Born in New York City in 1980, Shock's family moved to Tampa, Florida, when Shock was seventeen and already an accomplished musician. When his parents split up, Shock dropped out of high school and started getting into trouble. After landing in jail several times for petty drug dealing, Shock went back to school. After graduation, he moved to Oakland and formed Digital Underground.

When Tupac Amaru Shakur strode confidently into the presence of the wildly popular Shock G for an audition, "we [Digital Underground] were mixing down *Sex Packets*, our first album," Shock G later recalled. "Pac came in the studio, strictly business. He maintained eye contact with me the whole time," causing Shock to think, "Damn, this cat's intense."

But Tupac was more than intense; he was good. His rhymes struck Shock G with the clear message that there was something truly different about the intense "cat" who was asking him for a chance. A friendship based on strong mutual respect was born when, in commenting on Tupac's audition, Shock said, "Yeah, you tight. I'm a holler at you."

Tupac started off as Shock's roadie but he rapped at every turn, even while he went about his menial duties. It didn't take long for Tupac to make a name for himself as a talented professional with a strong work ethic. Leila slowly relinquished management of his career to Atron, but, author Michael Eric Dyson has noted in *Holler If You Hear Me: Searching for Tupac Shakur* that "she remained a crucial presence in his life."

Although Leila enjoyed having Tupac in the house, he was a typical teenager. He liked to play his music very loud and neighbors often complained. He started carrying video cameras wherever he went to ensure that, in the event of an encounter with the police, there'd be a visual record. He wanted incontrovertible proof of police brutality similar to that which had produced such public outrage in the case of Rodney King. On one occasion the police came to Leila's apartment to investigate a loud music complaint. As she apologized to the officers, Tupac mouthed off in the background, asking the officers if they were going to investigate the loud rock music that a neighbor often played.

"I was looking at him like please don't start anymore problems," Leila recalled. "I keep having problems already, ever since you got here."

In 1990, the song "Humpty Dance" was released on the album *Sex Packets* by the group Digital Underground. The song was an ode to the group's leader, Gregory E. "Shock G" Jacobs, who was also known as Humpty Hump, another stage name.

Shock G had Tupac Shakur on stage with him when he performed the Humpty Dance, gyrating enthusiastically to high-energy beats. In one memorable routine, Tupac and another dancer literally had their pants down so low that their underwear showed as they humped two mannequins.

Tupac's initial exposure to a broad audience offered the first glimmer of his potential as a performer and eventual star. He didn't question the stage routine but simply did his best in keeping with his stellar work ethic.

Humping a mannequin might not have been his choice for a stage debut, but the Digital Underground already had a reputation as a rap performance act that celebrated absurdity. This was mostly due to the fun-loving stage antics and partying persona of Shock G, who was described by music critic James Bernard as "hip-hop's split personality."

During DU shows, Shock G donned his trademark glasses with a bulbous prosthetic nose and became his flamboyant alter ego, Humpty Hump. Keeping in time and step with Humpty as he glided, hopped, jittered, and played across the stage was Tupac, matching him move for move, stride for stride, and bounce for bounce. They were doing what they loved and were having fun, but they were also doing a job and Tupac met the enthusiastic approval of his boss and the cheering crowds.

After Digital Underground's "Humpty Dance" became a hit, Tupac began touring with the group, which performed all over the United States and then went on to Japan. While on tour, he learned that Afeni was back on crack. "It fucked me up," he said. "I started blocking her out of my head."

The group's next album was *This Is an EP Release,* which followed the 1990 platinum-selling *Sex Packets.* Tupac got his big break on this album. He had been begging for a chance to show that he could do more than dance and work as a roadie, and Shock gave him a solo spot on the cut "Same Song." This was the first time Tupac Shakur debuted his rap skills to a large audience; he also appeared in the music video for the popular single.

In the video, Shakur appears as an African ruler sitting in his royal chair. He is carried by servants onto the stage, where he stands up and takes command of his surroundings. His rap is passionate and the back-and-forth patter between him and Shock G is funny and memorable.

Digital Underground and Tupac, performing "Same Song," garnered more exposure in the 1991 film *Nothing but Trouble*. The film starred Dan Akroyd, Chevy Chase, John Candy, and Demi Moore, signaling the group's and Tupac's rising fame.

Akroyd plays a gruesome judge in the strange town of Valkenvania. He takes great pleasure in hanging passersby for speeding violations, conducting his traffic court from a mansion located in the midst of a toxic waste dump. In the film, Digital Underground is being held by the judge and has to perform to win release. The song they perform is "Same Song." Like other DU performances, it is a party and even Akroyd, as the repellant, quirky judge, joins the music fest.

Tupac and Shock G formed a close collaborative relationship on *EP Release*. They enjoyed being in each other's presence and respected and admired each other's creative abilities and stage energy. And there was plenty of it.

Tupac's intensity sometimes flared into anger, usually when he perceived that people or circumstances were compromising the quality of the act. On one occasion, Tupac had to be restrained from physically assaulting the sound man for allegedly not working hard enough to ensure that all was in tip-top shape. On other occasions, Tupac directly challenged the creative reasoning, decisions, and processes of Shock G over issues ranging from the duties of specific DU members during a performance to their detailed placement on stage.

With each clash, Shock G asserted his authority as the group's leader, repeatedly firing Tupac and sending him home. But as tempers cooled, Shock and Tupac would be found out on the town, laughing and joking.

Tupac had already decided that if things with Digital Underground did not work out, he'd go to Atlanta and connect with the New African Panthers. But things did work out. Like caring elder brothers, Shock G and DU members took it upon themselves to help Tupac get himself established and secure.

"We were like family to him," Shock G later observed. "We got him his first apartment. He had no credit. He couldn't drive. He had no driver's license. So we used to have to work the applications. And we would all pitch in and borrow a credit card and cosign and did all the shit we had to do."

On his first visit to Tupac's new ground-floor apartment in a rough neighborhood, Shock G was appalled to discover that all of the lights were on, the windows were wide open, and the drapes pulled apart. "Pac, for real man, you're not getting the message," Shock gently admonished his friend. "You can't leave your windows wide open with all of these gold records and your jewelry laying out on the counters and stuff." Tupac agreed and then showed Shock the new AK-47 assault rifle that he'd just bought to handle any who might want to make Tupac's property their own.

The group eventually went on another tour, and Tupac returned months later with high hopes about his future as a rapper. What he didn't know was that his sister, thirteen-year-old Sekyiwa, had been taking care of herself. Afeni had abandoned her. To pay the bills, Sekyiwa let her twenty-two-year-old boyfriend live there and pay the rent from the money he made selling marijuana.

Once Tupac returned, Sekyiwa was sent to live with her Aunt Gloria in New York. He refused to have anything to do with Afeni, who by then was living with drug-using friends.

Just as Shock concerned himself with his friend's safety in the world, Tupac devoted himself to making sure that Shock was a success on stage. But he was also restless and wanted to break out on his own. It was time for Tupac to get a record deal for Tupac.

part three

STAR

sixteen

INTERSCOPE

igital Underground was signed to Tommy Boy Records, the company that had helped Queen Latifah early in her career. Atron Gregory approached Tommy Boy's A&R director, Monica Lynch, with Tupac's demo tape. Monica wasn't interested.

The demo tape wound up on the desk of Tom Whalley who arranged to meet Tupac. "He was incredibly personable and had a great sense of humor." Whalley gave the tape to his boss, Ted Field, co-owner of a struggling record company called Interscope. He passed it along to his teenage daughter who, along with liking the music, fell in love with Tupac's eyes. The endorsement from a teenager was all Field needed. He spoke with his partner, Jimmy Iovine, and soon Tupac got a record deal.

Field and Iovine were a tag team of entrepreneurial vision. Italian American Jimmy Iovine, the son of a longshoreman, was born on March 11, 1953, in Brooklyn, New York, and started his music career in the early 1970s. He worked as an engineer, a producer, and record company executive. He eventually expanded his endeavors to include film and television.

Jimmy Iovine owed much of his success to his father, Jimmy Iovine Sr., who worked in the tough world of longshoremen. He supported just about any interest that his son decided to pursue.

In 1973, the youthful Jimmy Iovine made his entry into the corporate music world at the Record Plant recording studio, eventually working with a number of influential artists such as the legendary John Lennon. He went on in 1975 to work as a recording engineer for Bruce Springsteen's *Born to Run*, and finally moved into producing in 1977 with a New Jersey band called Flame.

Iovine's production credits steadily added up, and his reputation as a star-making producer became solidly established. In 1976 he produced *Easter* for Patti Smith, an album that spawned a Top 40 hit single "Because the Night," coauthored by Smith and Bruce Springsteen. His collaboration with rocker Tom Petty in 1979, 1981, and 1982 yielded, respectively, stellar results with the albums *Damn the Torpedoes*, *Hard Promises*, and *Long After Dark*.

Iovine eventually established a personal and professional partnership with songstress Stevie Nicks in 1981, producing her first solo album, *Bella Donna*, which topped the charts. Nicks sought out Iovine again in 1983 for *The Wild Heart*. By 1984, Iovine had added U2 and their *Under a Blood Red Sky* to the list of artists and albums that he'd successfully produced.

Iovine's personal life took a nosedive in 1985 when Stevie Nicks succumbed further to drug addiction. In response, Jimmy drove himself deeper into his work and over the next five years produced albums for groups like Lone Justice (*Lone Justice*), Simple Minds (*Once Upon a Time*), the Pretenders (*Get Close*), Patti Smith (*Dream of Life*), and U2 (*Rattle and Hum*).

Overall, the 1980s were extremely good to Iovine, but with the arrival of 1990 he began distancing himself from music production as he turned his attention to a new enterprise, Interscope Records, which he cofounded with Marshall Field retailing fortune heir, Ted Field.

Although his birth name was Frederick Woodruff Field, he chose to go by Ted. On June 1, 1953, in Chicago, Illinois, Frederick "Ted" Field was born into the power and wealth that had been created by his grandfather, owner of the world's largest department store, Marshall Field & Company. After World War II, his grandfather sold the store to found a media empire whose centerpiece was the *Chicago Tribune*.

Among his many activities, Ted Field was best known as a television and film producer. His efforts resulted in memorable ventures like *Revenge of the Nerds* (1984), the TV movie *American Geisha* (1986), the miniseries *Murder Ordained* (1987), the film *Three Men and a Baby* (1987), and the raucously silly but highly popular *Bill and Ted's Excellent Adventure* (1989). However, it was the Interscope Records joint venture with Jimmy Iovine in 1990 that brought both men wealth and controversy.

The partners first contracted with Atlantic Records, a division of the powerful Time Warner media conglomerate, for distribution in a $30 million venture. They scored quick success with the Spanish-English (sung that way for the first time) hit single "Rico Suave" by Gerardo, released in 1991. That achievement was followed by a hit from Marky Mark & the Funky Bunch, a hip-hop group whose song "Good Vibrations" became a hit. Also in 1991 Interscope gave the hard-working, ambitious rapper Tupac Shakur a break.

Although Interscope was struggling financially when Tupac was signed, its willingness to take a chance testified to the company's efforts to position itself as "something of a maverick in the music business."

seventeen

2PACALYPSE NOW

When Tupac set out to create the album that would become *2Pacalypse Now*, he knew that he didn't want a straight party record. He also didn't want a collection of gangsta rap tunes, even though *Straight Outta Compton* by NWA had been a big hit. Instead, Tupac addressed social problems that folks in the ghetto dealt with every day. The first single, "Trapped," was released on September 25, 1991. It tackles thorny issues like the feeling of imprisonment when a person is penniless and living in the ghetto, and it then goes on to lament the fact that young black males are routinely stopped on the street by police who demand to see their identification without offering a legal explanation for the request. By the end of the song, a young black man, fed up with all the pressure, rebels against a police officer. The officer shoots him and he fires back. The cop falls dead and the kid goes on the run. He is seized and thrown into prison where he will remain trapped for the rest of his life.

The song was a hit and Tupac, elated by his good fortune, wasn't paying attention to traffic lights on October 17 as he jaywalked across an

Oakland street on his way to the bank. When he reached the entrance, two white male police officers, Alexander Boyovich and Kevin Rodgers, stopped him and demanded to see identification. He produced three items and the officers started teasing him about his strange name. Angry, Tupac demanded that they give him a ticket for the jaywalking and let him go on into the bank. According to Tupac, the officers replied that they could do whatever they liked to him or even arrest him on another charge.

Tupac cursed the officers and they threw him to the ground. He wore the facial scars for the rest of his life. They choked him until he lost consciousness and then kicked him awake before calling for a squad car that took him to jail. Forced to sit on the sidewalk in handcuffs while waiting for the car, Tupac felt humiliated. He had never been in trouble with police before. To make matters worse, the officers drove him around for two hours before finally dragging him off to jail. Because of his Digital Underground connection, the ongoing complaints by young black males against the Oakland Police Department, and the fact that he had a hit solo record in the stores, the incident made headlines.

Tupac couldn't believe it. He had lived in some of the country's most dangerous neighborhoods but had never seen the inside of a jail. Now, when he had worked hard and accomplished something, the public's first perception of him would be that of a lawbreaker. He appeared on BET and other media to tell his side of the story. On one occasion he asked the cameraman to zoom in so that the audience could see one side of his face. "These are learn to be a nigga scars," he said.

The bruises that Tupac sustained were grim reminders of the footage created by photographer George Holliday, who'd filmed police officers as they brutally beat Rodney King on March 3, 1991. King, an African

American parolee who was driving under the influence and maneuvering erratically, was pulled over by the California Highway Patrol after a high-speed chase. Fearing that he'd be returned to jail after he'd just served time for a robbery conviction, King had seen the police and fled, hitting speeds of around 115 mph. The police finally pulled him over and ordered King from the vehicle. A struggle ensued. Backup arrived. Moments later, King lay on the ground, curled into a fetal position as police officers pummeled him with nightsticks.

It was an example of what African American Los Angelinos had long complained about. Those complaints were often rejected with the result that charges were dismissed, ignored, or simply denied. But this time there was proof.

City officials were confronted with the awful truth that they'd been wrong.

The errors of the prosecutor's office proved to be just the tip of a judicial iceberg of systemic errors and cover-up. When the case went to trial, a jury of eleven white Americans and one Hispanic American acquitted the four police officers involved of all the charges but one. Black people were stunned. News programs from coast to coast had repeatedly shown the brutality inflicted on King. Millions of eyewitnesses were shocked to see an instance of the harassment that, for the black citizens of L.A., had become routine.

It was the last straw. The fuse of frustration that had been burning in the black community exploded into a devastating riot that left fifty-two dead, four thousand wounded, the community ravaged by looters and vandals, and costing over $500 billion in damage. As the smoke cleared and the nation wiped its brow to reflect on what had happened, the social rifts and fissures between blacks and whites came into view. The disparity of opinions provided a broad window of just how much work had yet to be accomplished in bridging the gap.

For blacks, the cruelty heaped on Rodney King and the subsequent acquittal of those responsible was proof of the systemic judicial repression and indifference that permeated so much of their lives. For many whites, the police had merely been doing their jobs as they served the public and maintained law and order.

On November 12, 1991, Interscope released 2Pacalypse Now. The tone was Lumbee Indians and their black cofighters join with the Black Panthers and set all their plans to music. It was raw. It was plain. It was focused. The songs, which were angry, accusatory, and filled with frustration, made sense to those living at the bottom of society, a place that Tupac knew all too well. "Rebel of the Underground" starts off talking about being on the wrong side of the establishment. Tupac then remembers that the people he truly cares about in places like the ghettos of Oakland "are backing me all the way." He notes wryly that while some folks would like to banish his message, the slums are creating a lot more rebels as he raps his truth. He notes that he has many suburban female fans he can sleep with if he wants to, even as their powerful fathers try to shut him down. In the end, he is determined to be heard and does not blame artists who keep their mouths shut in order to protect their careers.

In one of the less political songs, "Brenda's Got a Baby," he raps about a twelve-year-old girl impregnated by an older cousin. Cast aside by her family, she gives birth on her own and throws the baby into a dumpster. Hearing her baby cry, she retrieves it, and mother and child set out to cobble together some sort of rudimentary life. When Brenda resorts to prostitution, she is killed by a john and the listener is left wondering what became of Brenda's child. It is a heartbreaking song that endeared Tupac to young female fans, particularly those living in the foster care system or struggling with teenage pregnancy.

The album jolted mainstream America with raw, disturbing truths about the conditions confronting young urban black Americans and thrust Tupac into the crosshairs of the establishment. Critics were quick to charge him with being the personification of the problems he rapped about.

eighteen

JUICE

uice was a slang term used in the inner cities of the 1990s. Juice meant power, influence, and respect. To some poor and powerless people, particularly the young, obtaining juice in the neighborhood was everything. In the 1992 movie of the same name, Tupac played a troubled teenager named Bishop who lived with his grandmother and father.

It is never clear what happened to Bishop's mother, and his father (who was repeatedly raped in a penitentiary) sits in a catatonic state, staring at a television set. Bishop is constantly teased by the local gang leader about his father's past. What Bishop yearns for is respect. The drama revolves around Bishop and his three buddies (played by Omar Epps as Q, Jermaine Hopkins as Steele, and Khalil Kain as Raheem), who are all searching for juice in their own way.

The boys start out innocently enough by playing hooky and running around the neighborhood getting into mischief. But things take a dark turn when they decide to rob a store to gain respect from their peers. Bishop needlessly shoots the store owner and their lives spiral downward.

In a memorable scene, Q tells Bishop that he is crazy. Bishop replies, "You're right. I am crazy. But you know what? I don't give a fuck."

That line became associated with Tupac and he was never able to live it down.

On the set of *Juice*, Tupac's fellow actors were inspired by his work ethic. He stayed in character until he seemed to be channeling Bishop. In take after take, he insisted on striving for a perfect performance. It paid off. *Juice* was a hit. The Hollywood establishment also took notice of Tupac's superb acting skills and he received rave reviews. Janet Maslin of the *New York Times* wrote that Tupac was the "film's most magnetic figure" while Peter Travers of *Rolling Stone* magazine stated, "There's no denying his power as an actor."

In less than three years, Tupac had gone from homeless teenager to platinum-selling recording artist and movie star. With stardom came famous friends and invitations to parties in places he had never even dared to dream about. There were limousines, champagne, and plenty of women.

On the home front, Afeni had finished rehab and kicked her drug habit, but Tupac still had not completely forgiven her. Their relationship was strained but he took care of her and Sekyiwa. Tupac worked hard, partied hard, and reveled in his success.

Then trouble came calling again. On April 11, 1992, an attorney for a nineteen-year-old man named Ronald Ray Howard of Texas claimed that the music from *2Pacalypse Now* had caused his client to shoot a Texas Department of Public Safety trooper named Bill Davidson.

Davidson had stopped Howard in Jackson County, on Highway 59, for driving with a broken headlight. Howard, driving a stolen vehicle, shot Davidson in the neck and fled. A short couple of hours later, he was arrested and the 9-millimeter, hollow-point loaded pistol that he had in his possession was confiscated. Howard subsequently confessed to killing the state trooper and repeated his confession to a grand jury.

This tragedy did little to quell mainstream angst over the lyrics in 2Pacalypse Now. Even though the lawyer's attempt to attribute Davidson's actions to musical influence failed to convince the jury of Howard's innocence, it did further inflame an increasingly hostile faction that believed the worst about rappers.

Vice President Dan Quayle declared that 2Pacalypse Now had "no place in our society." Quayle would have done himself and the nation a far better service by focusing on the idea that something was desperately wrong in the urban hinterlands. In Gunshots in My Cook-Up, author Selwyn Seyfu Hinds notes that "no scouring brush applied to the mouths of rappers" could "clean up the truly profane conditions of America's inner cities." Nor could "they dispel the violence, patriarchy, and sexism this society has long thrived on. Those conditions existed ages before hip-hop spun into being and will exist long after, unless we apply meaningful change."

Tupac had filed a $10 million police brutality lawsuit against the Oakland police department over the jaywalking incident and they eventually settled with him for $42,000. Unfortunately, the problem with the police, Vice President Quayle's remarks, and his movie debut as Bishop in Juice marked Tupac with a wild outlaw image.

The people of Marin City were also angry with Tupac because of the way he described "the Jungle" during media interviews. He depicted it as a hopeless place where teenage pregnancy, drugs, and crime reigned supreme. True or not, inhabitants felt betrayed.

Theirs was a hard existence, and they knew from direct contact with Tupac that he was intimately acquainted with their daily hardships. For a time, those hardships had been his. It was those hardships—poverty, a dysfunctional home with a drug-addicted mother, and instability everywhere but at school—that had been prime motivators for Tupac's determination to get out. His acquaintances wanted the same, but life in the Jungle had taught them grim lessons of reality juxtaposed against the likelihood of fulfilling their own dreams. Many accepted that they might not see theirs come to fruition, but in Tupac they saw possibility and thought they could live through him.

"My boy Pac was always ambitious," friend Marku Reynolds observed. "He was eager. He was hungry. . . . He would eat rap, drink rap, and sleep rap, but it was just like another thing to me. I didn't take it seriously. It was another fad to me . . . but you could tell that he [Tupac] was going somewhere with it."

But before success, Tupac lived with friends when life was so dismal at home. Before success, Tupac stood nose to nose with challengers, holding his ground, demanding respect, prepared to fight for the cause of that moment. Before success, Tupac earned respect by rapping, taking frequent ass-kickings without complaint, and remaining loyal to his friends. Once he met the criteria for inclusion in the unforgiving Jungle, he had the backing of his friends who looked out for him and they expected the same from him. What they didn't understand was that he had been in the group but not one of them was in his heart. He did what he needed to make it through the day, but his inner eye was always on escape. He could laugh and joke with his friends, but Tupac was deadly serious about his goals.

In one media interview, Tupac, reflecting back on his days in Marin City and the Jungle, spoke bitterly as he noted that "niggas that wasn't shit and I knew it used to dis me. . . . But I didn't have no money and that's what used to fuck me up. . . . It be shitty, dumb niggas who had women, rides, houses, and I ain't have shit. . . . All through my time there they used to dis me. . . . I got love but the kind of love you would give a dog or a neighborhood crack fiend. They liked me because I was at the bottom."

Word got back to Tupac that his former neighbors were angry. He apologized. One of the old crew asked him to make up for his remarks by performing for free at the 1992 Marin City Festival. Tupac agreed. But he wasn't welcome.

A fight broke out and Tupac's entourage jumped in to protect him. Someone in the crowd fired a gun. The bullet hit a six-year-old boy in the head, killing him. Enraged, the crowd ran after Tupac and his friends. Tupac was forced to hide under a parked car until police arrived and order was restored.

Although Tupac and the members of his entourage were cleared of any criminal culpability, the people of the Jungle felt betrayed.

nineteen

T.H.U.G. L.I.F.E.

𝕴t wasn't the mother of all bad ideas, but it came close. When Tupac Shakur decided to launch his urban social reform movement under the banner of T.H.U.G. L.I.F.E., his image fell under intense scrutiny. The truth within the acronym—The Hate U Give Little Infants Fucks Everyone—was understood well enough by those who bothered to look beneath the surface message. But unfortunately for Tupac Shakur, when most Americans heard the word "thug" it conjured images that were consistent with the dictionary definition of the word: a cutthroat or ruffian; hoodlum. But Tupac failed to comprehend the historical and contemporary forces and institutions arrayed against him.

That the majority of Americans would have been ignorant of the message contained in T.H.U.G. L.I.F.E. was not surprising. The banner simply confirmed what they already felt about rappers anyway.

But members of the hip-hop community had always believed that black men had it within their power to make positive, lasting change. They believed that it would come in a variety of forms and would take

100

many hands and voices. Tupac Shakur was ready to lend his talent, voice, and passion to the cause. Given his painful upbringing, it was no surprise that Tupac was primed and ready to do his part in leading young black people into better days. Ending black-on-black violence was long overdue. Liberating the black community from the scourge of crack addiction and the dealers who sold the poison to their own people would constitute a miracle from God. And healing the rifts between black men, women, and children so that families could be strengthened, education pursued, and achievement cherished were actions that needed rapid implementation.

Unfortunately, his well-intentioned plan to achieve radical change was so ridiculous and counterproductive that even if it had worked, the black community would not have advanced an inch.

Tupac's plan for the T.H.U.G. L.I.F.E. was discussed with his stepfather, Mutulu Shakur, during a prison visit in 1992. Reclamation of the black community was surely a goal worth pursuing. But sadly for Tupac, he was up against a history that guaranteed a perversion of his intentions once he articulated them from beneath the dubious heading of T.H.U.G. L.I.F.E.

Black people's long experience in America offered numerous historical examples that the majority would resist sudden, radical change for the better within the black community.

In 1831, when Nat Turner and others had sought to throw off their bondage, their effort was called an *insurrection*. When Frederick Douglass liberated himself from the same miserable system he was declared a *fugitive*. When Rosa Parks refused to give up her bus seat and her dignity, she was deemed a *public threat*. When Malcolm X spoke truths about the daily violence endured by blacks in America, his message was cynically reinterpreted as a call for, well, *violence*. When Martin Luther King Jr. vowed to win civil rights for black people through love he was labeled a *communist* and enemy of the state.

These were the pitfalls that awaited Tupac as he ventured forth to announce that T.H.U.G. L.I.F.E. would be the new way.

If things went as they usually did, then America wouldn't get the true meaning of the message, and it didn't. If things went as they usually did, then America would spend little time plumbing the deeper meaning of the movement. America had other things to do and better ways to spend its time. No matter how much Tupac explained what was really behind the letters of T.H.U.G. L.I.F.E. dictionaries still defined thug as "cutthroat or ruffian; hoodlum."

"It's not thugging like I'm robbing people," Tupac later stated of his movement. "That's not what I'm doing. Part of being a [thug] is to stand up for your responsibilities and say this is what I do even though I know people are going to hate me and say 'It's so politically un-correct.'"

Tupac had so much respect in the black American ghettos that he was able to bring powerful gang leaders around to his way of thinking. In 1992, at an event called the Truce Picnic, the leaders of the Bloods and Crips, two of the nation's most notorious street gangs, agreed to live by the code of T.H.U.G. L.I.F.E. This new code of the streets was meant to curb the twin scourges of drugs and violence that were ravaging black neighborhoods.

The new rules were:

1. All new Jacks to the game must know: a) He's going to get rich. b) He's going to jail. c) He's going to die.
2. Crew Leaders: You are responsible for legal/financial payment commitments to crew members; your word must be your bond.
3. One crew's rat is every crew's rat. Rats are now like a disease; sooner or later we all get it; and they should too.
4. Crew leader and posse should select a diplomat, and should work ways to settle disputes. In unity, there is strength!

5. Carjacking in our Hood is against the Code.

6. Slinging to children is against the Code.

7. Having children slinging is against the Code.

8. No slinging in schools.

9. Since the rat Nicky Barnes opened his mouth, ratting has become accepted by some. We're not having it.

10. Snitches is outta here.

11. The Boys in Blue don't run nothing; we do. Control the Hood, and make it safe for squares.

12. No slinging to pregnant Sisters. That's baby killing; that's genocide!

13. Know your target, who's the real enemy.

14. Civilians are not a target and should be spared.

15. Harm to children will not be forgiven.

16. Attacking someone's home where their family is known to reside must be altered or checked.

17. Senseless brutality and rape must stop.

18. Our old folks must not be abused.

19. Respect our Sisters. Respect our Brothers.

20. Sisters in the Life must be respected if they respect themselves.

21. Military disputes concerning business areas within the community must be handled professionally and not on the block.

22. No shooting at parties.

23. Concerts and parties are neutral territories; no shooting!

24. Know the Code; it's for everyone.

25. Be a real ruff neck. Be down with the code of the Thug Life.

26. Protect yourself at all times.

As a sign of his commitment, Tupac eventually had T.H.U.G. L.I.F.E. tattooed across his midsection. Watani Tyehimba, a former Black Panther and childhood acquaintance was horrified: "What have you done?"

he asked. "We talked about it, and it became clear that he [Tupac] did it to make sure that he never forgot the dispossessed, never forgot where he came from. He was straddling two worlds. And he saw that we never make it as black people unless we sell out. He was saying that he never would."

Just as the name T.H.U.G. L.I.F.E. guaranteed its own misinterpretation, the street code it asserted proved problematic. No matter how much Tupac desired a different outcome, there was little likelihood that enduring virtue could be found in recommending principles that, for example, frowned upon selling drugs to pregnant women while implying that it was okay to sell them to women who weren't pregnant.

The code was supposed to be a manifesto of liberation when, in fact, it just established rules by which the black community was supposed to better endure its chaos and disintegration. For example, anyone informing the police of criminal activity would pay a heavy price: death. The message was that the black community was more interested in keeping criminals from getting caught rather than in eliminating crime.

Carjacking friends and neighbors was strictly forbidden. Did that mean terrorizing and carjacking black strangers was within the bounds of acceptability? Selling drugs to children, having children sell drugs, and selling drugs in schools were correctly forbidden; but those rules could have been improved if they'd simply forbidden selling drugs at all.

Under the new code, rather than having the police patrol, harass, and intimidate black people, that right that would henceforth be reserved for street toughs who recognize no laws but the ones they'd make up.

Civilians were declared off-limits as targets when gun battles should have been declared an obvious safety hazard for everyone. Harm to children would not be forgiven, but a certain amount of latitude was accorded to harming adults. Attacking family homes was frowned on. Did that mean it was okay to attack single apartment dwellers? Elders were declared untouchable for abuse as if such a rule were the grand dawning of new civilization.

On and on the code went: the flawed logic that sought to bring peace to the community without outlawing guns; the hypocrisy that frowned on drug dealing but tolerated drug abuse; the admonition to protect oneself at all times, which admitted that public safety could not be guaranteed, all underscored the deficient conceptual nature of T.H.U.G. L.I.F.E.

T.H.U.G. L.I.F.E., it seemed, was exactly what people assumed from the title: a life fit only for thugs. And this was the harmful program that Tupac embraced with all of his heart.

To love black people required doing all within one's power to urge them to stop hurting each other with drugs, guns, violence, and family disruption. Those objectives could not be reached by hiding behind pseudo-heroic rules of macho conduct, elements that had contributed to making life for black people so miserable in the first place. For someone of Tupac's stature to hold up these proposals as the means by which paradise would descend was to ensure that paradise was further delayed. And in this, Tupac failed.

Tupac failed to discern that his program stopped short of the truly revolutionary platform that had been written by Huey Newton and the original Black Panthers. Before their demise, the Panthers had begun resolving problems in the black community through a program of self-sufficiency.

For all of its good intentions, T.H.U.G. L.I.F.E accommodated lesser forms of chaos rather than rendering the critical element that had propelled Tupac through many of his darkest days: hope.

At the height of the campaign, Tupac had thousands of believers and the pressure became almost unbearable. He believed that his speeches to the gangs had put him on the government radar, and that frightened him.

Tupac had used focus, determination, and self-sufficiency to rewrite his own early hardship into an epic of success. Why couldn't he advocate the same for the people who lived in the ghetto? The answer was simple: he wanted to live up to his revolutionary name and background in order to make his family proud of him. He succeeded. Long after his death, some family members pointed to the T.H.U.G. LI.F.E. campaign as his greatest achievement.

twenty

THE WOMEN

The social, economic, political, and cultural trials and challenges of the 1980s became more debilitating in the 1990s. Eight years of the Reagan administration's smearing of the poor, the working poor, the unemployed, and the disabled had taken their toll. Writing in the *New Republic*, Robert Wright summed up those eight years by observing, "The fact that things worked out no worse than they did is either a tribute to the institutional sturdiness of the presidency or proof of the existence of God."

In the riveting 1991 film *New Jack City*, actor Wesley Snipes gave a chilling performance as Nino Brown, the ruthless leader of a Harlem drug ring (peddling crack cocaine) who strikes terror into the heart of the black community. Brown and his partner, G-Money, built a crack empire called CMB, Cash Money Brothers. Their turbulent rise to power, their vicious strangulation of the community's people, values, and harmony, and the chaotic unraveling of their pain-dispensing "business" echoed the frightful realities that had become routine throughout urban America at the start of the 1990s.

The 1980s crack plague that migrated into the 1990s brought incomprehensible levels of economic devastation and personal suffering to urban communities. The massive influx of black men into the nation's jails meant that most African Americans had a family member, friend, or acquaintance who'd been sucked into the labyrinth of the criminal justice system either as a perpetrator or victim.

Music and television productions began depicting social reality. Fox TV's *COPS* premiered on September 11, 1989, showing the dangers faced by uniformed police officers who used every means in their power to protect an unaware public from lurking dangers. The hapless citizens who cowered in communities besieged by drug dealing parasites eventually demanded action from public officials.

These were some of the social conditions that prevailed as Tupac's music career grew wings. Countless young people had only themselves to rely on when their elders embraced the crack pipe. Sekyiwa has said, "When my mom was using drugs I was in sixth grade. I went to school everyday. My mother wasn't home. My brother wasn't home for like months at a time. I still went to school everyday."

She also once said, "I've always been the shadow in the corner. I'm actually the heart in my family. My mother is the backbone. Pac is the catalyst. I'm the heart. I'm what keeps us together. My mom never taught me how to cook. She taught my brother how to cook, and I happened to be in the room when she did it. She never taught me about being a woman. She was telling Jada, when they were in high school. I just happened to be in the room listening to that."

His star rose fast and high, but from the moment he'd caught the public's attention, many wondered, and he let them wonder, if he was as crazy as he sometimes appeared to be. Who was the real Tupac? A bohemian, poetry-writing dreamer who read voraciously on the human condition. The Baltimore School of the Arts was the only place where

Tupac could be himself without fear of ridicule. When he was forced to leave the prestigious high school, he had already completed his college applications, so it is clear that he wanted to be in a space where he didn't have to hide his true nature. In his family and neighborhood, the real Tupac wasn't welcome. He had to appear "hard."

Tupac dated widely and across racial barriers. Women waited near backstage entrances hoping for a glimpse of him. Women hung around his Oakland apartment, calling through the door and offering to buy him food, drink, or anything else he wanted. It was a heady and exciting time for Tupac. Yet he still lacked self-confidence. Deep down inside, Tupac never believed that he was worth much and he hid that fact behind a fake bravado. The hotter his bad boy image became, the more women flocked to him.

He still had his old friend, Jada Pinkett. After graduating from the Baltimore School of the Arts in 1989, she had briefly attended college in North Carolina before heading west to seek stardom. Once in Los Angeles, she landed roles in TV series like *Doogie Howser* and *A Different World* before movie roles like *A Low Down Dirty Shame* and *Wood* started coming her way. He trusted Jada and Leila more than any other females he knew.

Although Tupac expressed himself rather tactlessly when dealing with a hostile press, his records kept selling. The way he saw it, people either understood where he was coming from or they didn't. People either backed him or opposed him (and he opposed them). People were either strong enough to help him bear the insanity, or they were weak and invited to be excused from his presence.

Somewhere in the roiling essence of Tupac's music he directed arrows of criticism to the innumerable events of police brutality that were all too real. But he also implored black people, at least in his early music, to do better, to straighten up, and to make sure that they were on the side of right so they could justifiably demand the same.

As Tupac's career soared, Leila watched closely, noting that his lyrics stayed true to views that he'd shared with her: "He felt that there
was no greater pain in this country at" the "time than the pain of black
America."

twenty-one

STRICTLY 4 MY N.I.G.G.A.Z.

upac symbolized the controversies and triumphs that defined the hip-hop generation. Simultaneously admired and castigated, Tupac and his music were deemed threatening and unacceptable by the establishment. The fact that his fan base was not just confined to the black ghettos but included white audiences as well infuriated many people. Tupac was unrepentant.

"I rap about fighting back," he declared.

Tupac's sophomore album, *Strictly 4 My N.I.G.G.A.Z.*, was released on February 1, 1993. Like his first one, it eventually went platinum. *Source* magazine called it "a combination of '60s black political thought and '90s urban reality."

"Holla If Ya Hear Me" excoriated sellouts, told Vice President Dan Quayle that Tupac wouldn't be silenced, and urged black men to "pump your fists if you're pissed."

Tupac took a break from the gloom and doom with "I Get Around," which is best described as a light and cheerful ode to youth, celebrity, rock stardom, and bachelorhood. He shares the rapping on this song with Shock G and Money B, two old colleagues from Digital Underground.

The song starts off with Tupac giving thanks to all men who keep their women from chasing him. He then shrugs off the problem of celebrity-chasing groupies as just something he'll have to deal with. The lucky women who get to sleep with him are warned, "You can't tie me down, baby doll, check it out, I get around."

Later, in "I Get Around," a groupie who chases him down and then is hesitant about sleeping with him exasperates him. He reminds her that he will only be in town for one night and that she needs to either hit the sheets or the door. Women he cares about are treated to "conversations on the phone til the break of dawn."

His critics pounced on this party song as well, calling it sexist and (because the word "ho" was used in reference to female groupies) offensive. The late Frankie Crocker, vice president of WBLS owner Inner City Broadcasting, said that the New York station, a favorite among blacks, was banning that song and others that were hateful to women. "We're taking the higher road. We're doing what is morally right," he said. On the West Coast, a group of Southern California community activists calling themselves Stop the Violence Increase the Peace lobbied radio stations to stop playing all songs containing the words nigga, bitch, or ho (whore). Rick Cummings, program director of KPWR radio, said, "We're really uncomfortable with censorship and the suppression of artistic expression, but we have to balance that with our responsibility to our listeners, many of whom are young people." Two weeks later he announced that KPWR was banning "Gin and Juice" and "What's My Name," both by Snoop Doggy Dogg, "It Was a Good Day," by Ice Cube, and "I Get Around," by Tupac Shakur.

But it was "Keep Ya Head Up" that won Tupac a permanent place in the hearts of poor black women. In that song Tupac acknowledged that black women had to deal with so many serious issues that sometimes they just wanted to drop their heads in their hands and roll around in pain. It described how they'd step out in their cutest clothes with smiles on their faces even though they were "dying inside." It also defended single mothers on public assistance who'd been vilified in the mainstream media as "welfare queens." It mostly communicated that women didn't have to accept abuse or ill treatment ("And if he can't learn to love you you should leave him cause sista you don't need him") just because they were poor.

The song's video was dedicated to Latasha Harlins, a black teenage girl who was shot to death in a grocery store by the Korean owner who thought she was trying to steal a bottle of orange juice. Her killer was convicted of voluntary manslaughter but served no time in jail. Tupac now had two hit albums under his belt. He'd starred in one movie and was filming another. He sold out concert engagements and appeared on television talk shows. He was rich. He was famous. He was a star. But something was clearly starting to go wrong.

On March 13, 1993, Tupac was in Hollywood to film a guest appearance on *In Living Color*, a popular variety show. When the director told everyone to take a break, Tupac and his friends hung out in a rented limo, which was parked in the Fox Television parking lot. The driver, David Deleon, said that the men started smoking weed in the car. When he asked them to stop, Tupac and one of the guys attacked him.

Tupac said that after words were exchanged, Deleon headed for the trunk of the car and he assumed that the driver was going to get a gun. Tupac was arrested for assaulting Deleon and released on $15,000 bail. Tupac later explained that "we didn't know if the guy was getting a gun or what." A judge agreed and the charges were dropped.

Less than a month later, Tupac was in Lansing, Michigan, performing at a concert. He ended up doing ten days in jail for taking a swing at a local rapper with a baseball bat.

His cousin, Jamala Lesane, says "Pac's immediate family—never mind the revolutionaries, but us—we were welfare recipients, ghetto, drug dealers and drug abusers. We were the no-hot-water, no-heat, no-Christmas, doped-up, drugged-out kind of family. Tom (Gloria's husband) was the only one ever working. We were lazy. Sheets hangin' up in the window. Tupac was the only one out of all of us who had the passion to get out there. . . . He worked hard to get where he was."

Instead of basking in his hard-earned success, Tupac was acting like a juvenile delinquent. The lines between the traumas of his past and the possibilities of his future were blurring into a painful reality of his present.

twenty-two

POETIC JUSTICE

John Singleton is the only African American ever nominated for a Best Director Academy Award. The film was entitled *Boyz N the Hood,* and it was released in 1991, when he was only twenty-three years old, which also made him the youngest person ever nominated for Best Director. Impressed by Tupac's acting performance in *Juice,* Singleton decided that he would be perfect for his upcoming film *Poetic Justice.*

Singleton needed someone who would drive himself and not be pretentious. He needed a man who wasn't star struck because the actor would portray Janet Jackson's love interest. Tupac showed up at the audition for *Poetic Justice* with his entourage, and they were all high—the first sign of trouble. But his charisma won over the decisionmakers, who noted that he had the look of a lover with a hard edge.

The movie was released on July 23, 1993. Tupac played Lucky, a young black postal worker who works hard and takes care of his young daughter even though he and the child's mother are no longer together. When Lucky realized that the tot was being reared in a dangerous and unstable environment, he took her to live with him. Lucky's life consists of

holding down his job, hanging out with his friend Chicago (played by
Joe Torry), and trying to win the affections of a depressed hairdresser
named Justice (played by Janet Jackson).

This is a road trip movie. Justice plans to attend a hair show in Oakland and Lucky agrees to drive her, Chicago, and Justice's best friend,
Iesha (played faultlessly by Regina King), in the postal truck. Lucky
believes that he and Justice will find romance on the trip and is upset
when he discovers that winning Justice won't be easy. The trip to Oakland produces tension, comedy, and tragedy as the four travelers come
to terms with what is and isn't working in their lives.

Tupac's behavior and language were too volatile for some on the
movie set, especially the distinguished Maya Angelou, who had a small
part in the film. Years later, she recalled, "Years ago I did a movie called
Poetic Justice and there was a young man . . . the first day he cursed so
I couldn't believe it. I walked around and behind him, trying to ignore
him, but the second day he and another young black man ran to each
other and they were about to fight. Hundreds of extras started to run
away but one black man walked up to the two young men and I walked
up and I took one by his shoulder. I said, 'Let me speak to you, honey.'
I finally calmed him down and I said, 'Do you know how much you are
needed? Do you know what you mean to us? Do you know that hundreds of years of struggle have been for you? Please, baby, take a minute.'
I put my arm around him. He started to weep. His tears came down.
That was Tupac Shakur. I took him and walked him down into a little
gulley and kept his back to the people so they wouldn't see him and I
used my hands to dry his cheeks. And I kept talking to him sweetly."

"Tupac probably spent a lot of time being afraid and overcompen-
sated with his tough guy persona so that no one would know," Dr. Sonja
Trent-Brown has suggested.

"He was a wild cat," John Singleton later noted. "But he was twenty
years old, he was making a movie with Janet Jackson, and three years

previously he had been practically homeless. Of course he was going to act up. He was a kid. All the weed he can smoke, every girl wants to sleep with him, every cat wants to be cool with him. You think you wouldn't lose your mind?"

There were other reasons, however, for Tupac's antsy behavior on the set, especially when the crew started filming in Oakland. His former neighbors from Marin City watched the action from behind the police barricades and they were brutal. For many of them, the sight before their eyes was too hard to believe. Just a short time before, they'd known Tupac as a desperate, struggling vagabond. Now he had suddenly reappeared on a movie set, acting alongside Janet Jackson.

Tupac was going in and out of his trailer and interacting with fawning publicists, doting makeup people, and slavish wardrobe consultants. For his former neighbors it was too much. In their minds, the once starving and homeless teen, son of a neighborhood crack head, had become a snooty, smug, and uppity traitor who'd forgotten his roots. They hurled jealous insults and epithets at him as he passed by the barricades. Tupac, still too insecure to let the tongue lashings simply bounce off him, took them to heart.

The other actors could hear the painful taunts and Tupac felt humiliated, but he kept working. His focus and dedication to the job also carried him through difficult times with Janet Jackson. On the set, they were barely cordial. For any kissing scenes, so the story goes, she insisted that Tupac first get an AIDS test. The request strained his patience and he refused.

Movie critics lauded Tupac's performance. The *Washington Post* said, "Shakur is wonderful too, with an immensely appealing, laidback sexiness." *Entertainment Weekly* said, "Tupac Shakur, who was so startling as the heavy-lidded sociopath in Ernest Dickerson's *Juice*, makes the ardent Lucky a complex and compelling figure." *The New Yorker* magazine said, "The only live wire is Shakur, with his deep wariness of life, who has a couple of sprightly scenes that prod the picture awake." New York's *Amsterdam News* said, "It's Shakur's charismatic personality and his ability to show sensitivity and emotional vulnerability on screen that helps make this movie exceptional." To top it off, Tupac was nominated for an NAACP Image Award in the lead actor category for his role in the film.

Before the film's release, Tupac and Singleton decided to hang out in Atlanta. They were in town for the black college student spring break celebration known as Freaknik to promote the film. While cruising up and down famed Peachtree Street, with his entourage trailing him in other cars, Tupac listened over and over to a song entitled "Party and Bullshit" by a relatively unknown rap artist.

Tupac played the song, rewound the tape, played it and rewound again, getting more excited each time he listened to the new rapper's terrific flow. He decided that no matter what, he had to meet the person who displayed such great storytelling skills.

The newcomer called himself Biggie Smalls.

twenty-three

PUFFY

$\mathcal{S}$ ean "Puffy" Combs, born in Harlem on November 4, 1969, a one-
time Howard University student and concert promoter, started
off at Uptown Records as an intern to Andre Harrell. Combs eventually
worked with entities like Jodeci, Heavy D & the Boyz, and Mary J. Blige.
He'd done a good job, but there'd been trouble along the way, notably
in December 1991 when Combs coordinated with the City College of
New York to host a basketball game with rap stars as a benefit for AIDS
awareness for the AIDS Education Outreach Program.

On the day of the event, chaos erupted when people standing in line
noticed others sneaking in through a second entrance and tried to force
their way in. Efforts to control the breakdown were fruitless. People
were trampled and nine were killed. A public outcry was raised after
it was determined that the event had been knowingly oversold. The
media, already lambasting Combs, further discovered that there was no
such thing as the AIDS Education Outreach Program.

In the days following the event, Combs spent a lot of time crying,
pacing, and talking with friends on the phone. He also turned to God.

He had little choice, since he was contemplating suicide and getting threats from persons who wanted to help him exit from the earth. Andre Harrell enlisted the assistance of high-profile lawyers to help in the defense. It was to no avail. Years later in 1998, a court ruled that Combs was partially responsible for the deaths.

Disaster did not stop Combs from moving ahead with his plans. He continued developing artists like Father MC and Jodeci. He gathered together his first entourage, ensuring that they projected the tougher image that hip-hop had assumed. He dyed his hair different colors, bought a white BMW with sparkling rims, and started wearing his sweatpants with one leg rolled up to the knee.

At parties at Andre Harrell's house, Combs flitted from guest to guest, introducing himself and making contacts. His one-track mind kept him focused on the mission to realize his dream: Bad Boy Records.

Combs sensed the pulse of hip-hop and the attitudes and expectations of people making fashion in the streets, and the look he crafted for Mary J. Blige won over the public. The single "Real Love" soared to number seven on the pop chart. Her album *What's the 411*, which was released on July 28, 1992, took the industry by storm, selling 2 million copies and being ranked at number thirty on *Village Voice*'s listing for the top 40 albums of that year.

Mary's success was gratifying, but Combs was looking forward to launching Bad Boy Records. He had been responsible for the success of Uptown. He'd learned much from Andre Harrell and was appreciative, but the time for merely talking about the dream of Bad Boy Records was coming to an end. Tensions between the two increased and Harrell had already responded by promoting the problematic Combs to be vice president of A&R, one of the youngest to ever hold that position. Following that, Harrell announced that Uptown would "host Puffy's new management, record, and production company." That didn't happen.

Artists were grumbling that Combs tried repeatedly to get his name listed alongside their songwriting credits. If so, he stood to profit from the publishing rights. He also lengthened the list of his own accomplishments to show future employers. And there was more.

Combs allegedly demanded to have his name appear "wherever Harrell had his listed, and developed a reputation for being a tyrant in the studio." There were complaints about his booking expensive studio time and showing up late, if at all. The bills Combs ran up put Harrell in a tough spot with MCA (his parent company) executives who were rapidly losing their sense of humor about Combs. Harrell wanted to keep Combs tied to Uptown since he'd been good for the company, but he also needed to put some distance between Combs and the company's budgets. One way of doing that was to back the launch of Bad Boy Records.

Combs had also become increasingly difficult to work with. Rumors circulated that Combs had not only been undermining and insulting Harrell behind his back but had gotten bold enough to do so in public, allegedly making comments like "You wouldn't be shit without me." Enough was enough, and Harrell fired Combs.

Combs's alleged boast about his value to Harrell and Uptown didn't stop him from crying for a couple of days after his firing. The tears flowed even faster when Harrell kicked him out of his New Jersey home, forcing Combs to move back in with his mother in Westchester. He remained undaunted, however, and soon set up his own company.

Combs let it be known far and wide that he was looking for a distributor. Harrell publicly supported Combs, and other black execs did also. Through that network, L. A. Reid, the producer who ran Arista-distributed LaFace Records, put Combs in contact with Clive Davis, a powerful figure in the music industry.

Davis met with Combs and found him to be well grounded. The two men clicked. Davis saw in Combs someone he could mentor. With a $15 million investment in Combs's enterprise, Davis agreed to back Combs with the stipulation that Combs spend time with him each month so he could teach his protégé the business.

Puffy would eventually change his nickname to Diddy, become a superstar in his own right, and impact the world of rap music, fashion, and pop culture in far greater ways than he could have imagined.

twenty-four

BIGGIE

H is mother had plans for him, but he had a vision of his own. He possessed all of the material comforts he could desire and was showered with more parental concern than he'd ever be able to absorb. But still, for Christopher Wallace, a.k.a. Biggie Smalls, a.k.a. The Notorious B.I.G., it wasn't enough.

Mother's dreams for her son were a poor substitute for the excitement he found on the streets. Warm food, nice clothing, soft blankets, the latest toys and video games, a stable home, and summers spent on the island of Jamaica couldn't compete with the dangers, risks, and inherent instability of his chosen profession: crack dealer. Exhortations to follow a straight and narrow path to middle-class respectability were trumped by the promise of an easy road to astronomical riches.

Finally Biggie's mother, Voletta, gave up. Another black male, her one and only son, was hanging out in the streets. It wasn't the first time that her heart had been broken.

According to her memoir entitled *BIGGIE*, Voletta had come from Jamaica to America for a better life. New York was all it had been rumored to be: big, juicy, exciting, full of opportunities for work, life, and love. Voletta found work. In Selwyn George Letore she found romance.

He was charming and smooth. He said whatever he felt that she needed to hear. When she got pregnant, it should have been a happy time, but they argued a good deal.

Voletta told her good friend Lauriece how Selwyn had blown up at her when she said that she wasn't ready to have a baby. "He asked me if I was too good to have his baby."

"How dare he speak to you like that!" Lauriece said. "What a dirty bastard!" adding, "Voletta, he's married."

Lauriece shared the rest of Selwyn's story. He'd been lying all along. He had a family in London, England. Voletta had been his midlife fling, and he'd strung along the naive Jamaican girl until it had gotten too uncomfortable.

"I had never been so angry and shocked," Voletta recalled. "I felt so stupid. And I wanted to kill somebody. Actually, I wanted to kill Selwyn! Married! I felt so used. I felt that he had gotten away with so much. The hate just swelled and festered throughout my entire body."

Christopher George Letore Wallace was born on May 21, 1972, in the Bedford-Stuyvesant section of Brooklyn at a pivotal time in musical and American history. His generation would be the last to remember what black music sounded like before hip-hop.

Unlike Tupac, Christopher was well cared for. "I made sure my son had an education, a good mattress, clean sheets, good quality clothes, and I gave him quality time," Voletta once explained, stressing that Christopher "wasn't the pauperized kid he made himself out to be" in the rap world.

Voletta had little use for George Letore, and Christopher had even less. Years later, when asked about his father, he responded, "Don't know him and I don't want to know him. I don't even remember that cat. . . .

I've seen pictures. He looks like a lame. I don't need that cocksucker for nothing."

At the age of ten he fell off a city bus, breaking his leg in three places. Voletta sued the City of New York and settled for a cool five figures. Once the legal fees were paid, she put a nest egg in the bank for Christopher's college education, dreaming big dreams for her boy.

Young Christopher was like other kids; but then again, he wasn't. He'd invite neighborhood kids over to play video games but he'd charge them a quarter. Voletta tolerated her son's unusual "business" since it kept him off the streets where kids were stealing and getting mixed up in violence. When he was twelve, he started selling drugs, not out of need but as a matter of choice.

Christopher's hanging in the streets and selling drugs were early acts of rebellion. At one point, he told his mother that he no longer wanted to go to Queen of All Saints School, where he had to wear a uniform. "He just wanted to be a regular kid." His mother finally allowed him to transfer to Westinghouse High School where there was essentially no discipline. "The student body—which included Trevor 'Busta Rhymes' Smith and Shawn 'Jay-Z' Carter—seemed to have the upper hand."

Before he became a drug dealer, Christopher had ideas of becoming a commercial artist. The money of the streets shattered that aspiration: "After I got introduced to crack—commercial art? Nigga, please" Wallace later mused. For twenty minutes of work on the street he could "get some real paper. . . . I didn't want no job. I couldn't see myself getting on no train for shit. I didn't want to work in no barber shop, I didn't want to do no restaurant. I wanted to sell drugs!"

And sell drugs he did, with a coldhearted practicality. "We used to have this rule that was, we ain't serving to no pregnant ladies," Wallace later said. "And there was a pregnant lady who used to come see us every day from Jersey that used to want, like, ninety capsules. I'm like, fuck it.

I mean if I don't give it to her someone else will. It ain't like she gonna go home and be like 'well Biggie didn't give it to me, I'm going to sleep.' She's gonna get high. So I'm going to handle my business. And niggas was like 'yo, you foul.'"

Wallace was a study in contrasts. He'd sell drugs to his neighbors but lecture his friend and sidekick James "Lil Cease" Lloyd about the virtues of staying in school. His mother worked hard to provide for him, but he preferred the streets. He was arrested once for selling drugs and was released because he didn't have a record. Then he was arrested again for parole violation. And he was almost arrested yet again for selling drugs, this time in no-nonsense North Carolina, which would have sent him to jail for fifteen years.

In 1992, Biggie was hoping for a record deal. He was known as the best rapper in his neighborhood and wanted to try for the big time. However, he couldn't stand rejection and didn't want to run around from label to label trying to get someone to listen to a tape. So he challenged his friend Bonz, who had contacts in the record business, to a game of dice called Cee-Lo. If Bonz won, Biggie would walk away and try another route to fame. If Biggie won, Bonz would use his influence to get Biggie started in his new career.

Biggie won and, not long after, Bonz used his contacts to land him a meeting with Puffy.

Soon after Biggie Smalls had signed with Uptown, Combs, doing his usual best to craft the image for his new artist, told Biggie that he'd have to stop selling drugs. But conditions at Uptown had gone from tense to hostile. Some employees had sided with Andre Harrell in desiring to follow a more traditional vision for music whereas others felt Puffy had a better sense of the market.

Biggie agreed to stay off the streets and Puffy went to work on his album. Everything was going well until Puffy got fired. Biggie couldn't believe it. "Party and Bullshit" had been a great single that had put him on the map. He had been so close to getting an album out. Now the rug had been snatched out from under him.

Biggie was depressed after being released by Uptown and had taken to drinking and staying high on weed. Associates taunted him, declaring that his music career had ended as fast as it started. Through it all, Combs stressed that Biggie had to stay clean and stay out of trouble or else "I'm never f**king with you again." Biggie obeyed . . . for the moment.

With his music career seemingly over, Biggie went to North Carolina, rented an apartment with some associates, and resumed selling drugs. Combs called Biggie and pleaded with him not to destroy his life, stressing that if he came back from North Carolina, he'd have a check waiting for him.

Bad Boy Records was officially in business.

Biggie went on a short promotional tour and ended up in Maryland, where he performed "Party and Bullshit." Tupac was in the audience, waiting for a chance to meet him. Cease recollected, "He said Pac was loving that shit. He stepped to Big like, 'what up, Big? I like your shit.'"

Biggie was flattered by Tupac's attention. After all, he was one of the most famous men in the entertainment industry. They partied that night, and the next morning Biggie heard a knock on his door. He opened it and there stood Tupac "smiling, with a bottle of Hennessy cognac in his hand."

Upon his return from Maryland, Biggie told Lil Cease, "Dawg is real. I gave him my number and told him when he come up here, we'll kick it." True to his word, Tupac came to Brooklyn. "A white limo pulls up on the block," Lil Cease recalled. "Pac jumps out," and the "hood's going crazy."

The bond between the two rappers was genuine. According to Cheo Hodari Coker's biography of Biggie, entitled *Unbelievable,* Tupac presented Biggie with not only an elder in the rap game but someone who'd survived the "the tumultuous childhood and abject poverty that Biggie rapped about but never actually lived." Biggie presented Tupac with someone who was "an artistic genius as well as someone who rolled with real thugs—gun toting outlaws with two feet in the street life."

The two enjoyed each other's company and soon their entourages began hanging out together as well. Tupac felt that Biggie was a true friend, someone he could trust. All hell would break lose when he was told by people he trusted that Biggie had betrayed him.

twenty-five

A SHOOTING IN ATLANTA

It was the middle of the night. Tupac and his entourage were driving along when they came upon two white men harassing a black motorist at an intersection. And this was happening in Atlanta, the so-called black mecca. As Tupac watched the black motorist being badgered, it seemed that the old southern rules were in full play.

Years of conditioning demanded that he do something, so he intervened. Words were exchanged. Tempers flared and shots were fired. The two men harassing the motorist were hit. Tupac had no way of knowing that the two men, Mark and Scott Whitwell, were off-duty police officers. Tupac was arrested on two counts of aggravated assault and released on bail.

Later in court, the Whitwells accused Tupac of taking the first shot at them. Witnesses, some of them white, who had been at the intersection told a different story. An intoxicated Mark Whitwell had pulled his weapon first, they said. Tupac insisted that he was only trying to assist a citizen whom he thought was about to be beaten or robbed. Once it was proven that Mark Whitwell fired first, Tupac's lawyers contended that he'd acted in self-defense. Whitwell's case became even weaker when an investigating detective stated that the officer's report had included the observation that "niggers came by and did a drive-by shooting."

There were also allegations that the two off-duty policemen had been drinking and acting belligerent prior to the incident. And then the prosecution's own witness testified that the gun one of the officers had used against Tupac had been seized in a drug bust and then stolen from an evidence locker.

Mark Whitwell was subsequently charged with aggravated assault. The charges against Tupac were dropped and the case was over. Tupac was glad to be alive and free. Most who knew Tupac also felt that his frequent run-ins with the law were the least of his desires. It made *no* sense for *any* black man who'd ever dealt with the police to purposely invite their attention.

Maurice Harding (Mutulu's biological son from his first marriage), who often performed with Tupac under the stage name Mopreme, was with Tupac that night: "We were all coming back from Clark University in Atlanta. We had just finished performing. We were going back to the hotel to party. There were two cars. Tupac was in the first car. I was in the second car. There were these two white officers harassing a black man that wasn't doin nothing. Tupac just jumped out of his car, went over and asked what the problem was. They told him to mind his business and get back in his car, which he did. Then they walked over to the car and smashed the window with one of the guns they had. That's when Pac got out and he dropped down to one knee and he shot them both in their butts. He could have just said hell I don't know that guy. Let me go upstairs and mind my business but he helped out a stranger. He didn't know that guy from nowhere. He had a bad side but I saw the good side. I saw the side that a lot of us blacks don't do and that is to help out a stranger cuz I know a lot of artists who would have just drove right by, went upstairs and had a nice time."

The law enforcement community was furious. Not satisfied with simply recording anticop songs, rappers apparently intended to act out the songs as well.

Overnight Tupac became a legend in the black community: a black man who had shot two white cops in the state of Georgia and lived to tell the tale.

Although Tupac may have felt that he was now the biggest and baddest that Lumberton or the black power movement had ever produced and therefore worthy of the family approval that he had always craved, people who had worked in the civil rights movement and the Black Panther Party were not cheering at all. They suspected that rogue forces in the government would soon get even with Tupac, and they were very afraid for him.

twenty-six

NEW FRIENDS

*I*n late 1993, when Tupac was in New York City filming *Above the Rim,*
he started making new friends, notably Jacques "Haitian Jack" Agnant, a Queens-based music promoter and true creature of the streets.
He and Tupac met while the rapper was researching his role of Birdy
for *Above the Rim.* From Tupac's perspective, being in the company of a
supposed bona fide gangster was thrilling. It was also dangerous. Word
on the street (which Tupac initially did not believe) was that Agnant
was also a government snitch.

Haitian Jack loved flashy clothes, flashy cars, and dropping names of
famous people. He traveled in all of the right circles, went to all of the
right parties, and used his showbiz connections to further his business.

When it came to that "business," Jack didn't play games. Derrick
Parker, a former NYPD cop who worked in the elite Gang Intelligence
Division, says that Jack "was famed for . . . his fearlessness. Agnant
wasn't afraid to run up on anyone." He ran a good business this way.
Agnant told Parker, "My thing is robbing drug dealers. The drug dealer,
see, he isn't going to call the police."

With the way crack and those who pedaled it had ravaged society by the 1990s, anyone who had the spine to jack a dealer was tough in a way that even tough guys might've found difficult to comprehend.

Russell Simmons said that "the niggers he [Tupac] hung with from Queens were rough. How rough? People whom I think killed people, whom I think had bodies, were scared of the crews Tupac rolled with from Queens."

Tupac later related that at the time, he was "hanging around these dudes—and I'm picking up their game. I didn't have to dress with a hoodie to be a thug. So I was dressing like they were dressing. They took me shopping, and that's when I bought my Rolex and my jewels. They made me mature. They introduced me to all these gangsters in Brooklyn. They was showing me all these guys who I needed to know to be safe in New York."

The fact that Tupac equated draping himself in jewelry and the company of real gangsters with manhood is troubling. Was he still looking for Legs, the gangster daddy figure whose death had so devastated him many years ago?

Biggie later claimed that he watched from a troubled distance as Tupac got closer to Agnant and his crew. He warned him to be careful, watch his step, and not be so trusting of his new friends. Tupac didn't stop associating with them, and Biggie, who was just beginning to make real money as a rapper, said he figured that Tupac simply preferred to hang out with rich men like Agnant. Feeling that he was unable to compete with Agnant's lifestyle, he decided to just have fun whenever Tupac showed up and forget about Tupac's other friends.

twenty-seven

THE BEGINNING
OF THE END

On November 14, 1993, less than a month after the shooting in Atlanta, Tupac went with Haitian Jack to the popular New York
night spot Nell's. A young woman named Ayanna Jackson was at the
club that night with a friend. The nineteen-year-old said that the friend
introduced her to Tupac's friends, Nigel and Trevor. They in turn introduced her to Tupac.

Later on, Tupac would say that he and the young woman danced and
then she gave him oral sex "in a dark corner of the club." She would
counter that Tupac pulled up his shirt, took her hand, traced it down his
chest and sat it on top of his erect penis. He then kissed her and pushed
her "head down on his penis, and in a brief three-second encounter,"
her "lips touched the head of his penis." The two then left the club together and had consensual sex in his hotel room.

Four days later, on November 18, 1993, Ayanna Jackson returned to
Tupac's $750-a-night suite at the Parker Meridian Hotel. Agnant was
there, along with Charles "Man Man" Fuller (Tupac's road manager)

and another man who has never been identified. Biggie was there too, but when Jackson arrived, he got up and left. Once she arrived, Agnant fixed drinks for everyone. Tupac and Jackson went into the bedroom.

Tupac would recall that all he was thinking about at that moment was getting another blow job. "So we get in the room, I'm laying on my stomach, she's massaging my back. I turn around. She starts massaging my front. This lasted for about half an hour. In between, we would stop and kiss each other. I'm thinking she's about to give me another blow job. But before she could do that, some niggas come in, and I froze up more than she froze up. If she would have said anything, I would have said, 'Hold on, let me finish.' But I can't say nothing, because she's not saying nothing. How do I look saying, 'Hold on'? That would be like I'm making her my girl."

Tupac said that he got up and walked out of the room. He said that he went out to the couch in the living room. High on weed and liquor, he fell asleep. He said that when he awoke, he found Jackson crying hysterically. "Why you let them do this to me . . . I came to see you. You let them do this to me . . . This is not the last time you're going to hear from me."

Jackson went downstairs and called the police.

Ayanna told an entirely different story: "He fell onto the bed and asked me to give him a massage. So I massaged his back, he turned around, and I started massaging his chest. Just as we began kissing, the door opened and I heard people entering. As I started to turn to see who it was, Tupac grabbed my head and told me, 'Don't move.' I looked down at him and he said, 'Don't worry, baby, these are my brothers and they ain't going to hurt you. We do everything together.' I started to shake my head . . . No, no, Pac, I came here to be with you. I came here to see you. I don't want to do this. I started to rise up off the bed but he brutally slammed my head down. My lips and face came crashing down hard onto his penis, he squeezed the back of my neck, and I started to gag. Tupac and Nigel (an alias used by Haitian Jack) held me down."

Jackson agreed that Tupac then left the room. When she eventually saw him again, he was lying on a sofa.

The police arrested all of the men.

Shock G said, "It is truly absurd to think that anybody in the hip-hop game with even mild celebrity status has to rape anybody." Shock apparently did not understand that rape is about power and control. Celebrity, money, or unlimited access to willing women had nothing to do with it.

Tupac's fans were shocked and disgusted. Entertainment executives ran for cover. By the end of 1993, Sony execs were pushing hard for John Singleton to drop Tupac from the cast of *Higher Learning* even though the lead role had been written for him. He'd become, in a manner of speaking, radioactive. Singleton was miffed, but there was little he could do as Sony, not wanting a part of the controversy, took a pass on Tupac.

Treach, from the rap group Naughty by Nature, says that during filming for *Above the Rim*, "people in the street yelled 'ah-hah (about the rape), you got caught out there.' That hurt him. That cut him down."

The wolves were circling, but Tupac still had friends who cared for him enough to tell him the truth of where he'd gone wrong. Jada Pinkett Smith recalls that she chided Tupac for leaving Ayanna Jackson in the bedroom with the other two men.

Tupac and Jada had remained close ever since their days at the Baltimore School of the Arts. When they hung out, he always made sure that she was safe. Now she scolded Tupac, telling him that he should have protected Ayanna Jackson no matter what. "If that . . . had happened to me," Smith said, "he would have killed somebody."

Jada's opinion meant everything to him. She had always been on his side. Not this time. After Jada's tongue-lashing, Tupac was crushed. He finally got it. Jada believed him when he denied raping Jackson, sodomizing her, or forcing her to give him oral sex. Yet she still felt that he was wrong and deserved punishment for leaving Jackson in the bedroom: "He understood that, and that was part of what ate at his soul."

Tupac had also stayed close to Leila Steinberg. She says, "Pac called me crying. Pac wasn't afraid to cry. That [rape charge] crushed him. You know sometimes it's about the company you keep. Pac's company was his downfall."

When friend and boxer Mike Tyson heard about Tupac's predicament, he wasn't surprised. He had also warned Tupac about Agnant. "I had already got a call from Mike Tyson saying 'Pac don't hang with Jack, he's bad news,'" Tupac shared later. "But I thought Tyson was being paranoid, so I was like, 'I'm not going to leave Jack until I see it for myself.'"

As he awaited trial, the storms from the incident with Ayanna Jackson ripped across the landscape of Tupac's world. He and Biggie were still friends but his relationship with Jack had chilled. He began wearing a bulletproof vest.

When Tupac arrived at a Puffy Combs party and saw Jack Agnant and his crew in the midst of Biggie's entourage, he was stunned. "I was hurt," Shakur later confessed. "I was like, 'I'm going to trial. I'm probably going to get convicted, and this nigga's showing up at a party with champagne, hanging with Biggie.' I was like, 'Damn, he's just bouncing from rapper to rapper.'"

Why was Biggie now friends with Agnant after warning Tupac away from him?

At the party, Biggie greeted his old friend with affection and introduced him to his wife, Faith Evans, whom he'd married sometime earlier. It seemed odd to Tupac that two people from Brooklyn, Biggie and Iron Mike Tyson, had warned him about the same man. It seemed odd that Biggie was now partying with that same man.

At the party, Tupac did not acknowledge Agnant's presence. This went against an ancient gangsta code, which dictates that enemies have to make eye contact and give each other a brief nod. Tupac played it his way and kept on talking to Biggie without adhering to the code. Perhaps he thought that his celebrity would protect him from any consequences. Perhaps he was too angry about his circumstances to care about what might happen next.

Tupac eventually claimed that "even though I didn't like them, I used to pretend. But now I couldn't pretend no more, because I knew they were snakes. When I saw them with Biggie, that's what let me know they were snakes. I was like, 'damn, they just bounce to the next nigga.' They weren't sending me any money. They weren't trying to help me through my charges, even though it was them that set me up. I was through with these niggas."

Tupac was through with Agnant and Hollywood was through with Tupac.

Christmas 1993 was silent and depressing for Tupac. Would he get convicted? Was his career over? Did his fans really believe that he raped and sodomized a woman? Who was Ayanna Jackson and would she have appeared in his life if he hadn't shot the two Atlanta cops? There were no answers to the troubling questions. All he could do was lie low and await the New Year.

No matter what happened, the horrible accusations had forever tarnished his love-for-my-black-people image. Worse, the situation began to change his personality. His talent would remain and he continued to be kind and generous to his family, but eventually his spirited persona would recede, leaving a bitterness in its wake.

twenty-eight

ABOVE THE RIM

What on earth was Tupac thinking? The last thing he needed to do was hit someone, but that's exactly what he did when directors Albert and Allen Hughes dropped him from the cast of the 1993 film, *Menace II Society*.

"They was doin' all my videos," Tupac said. "After I did *Juice*, they said, 'Can we use your name to get this movie deal?' I said, 'Hell, yeah.' When I got with John Singleton, he told me he wanted to be 'Scorsese to your De Niro. For starring roles I just want you to work with me.' So I told the Hughes brothers I only wanted a little role. But I didn't tell them I wanted a sucker role. We was arguing about that in rehearsal. They said to me, 'Ever since you got with John Singleton's shit you changed.' They was trippin' cuz they got this thing with John Singleton. They feel like they competing with him."

After this exchange, the Hughes brothers probably decided against moving forward with their project as planned, and they dropped Tupac from *Menace II Society*. He said they didn't tell him he was fired and he heard the news on MTV along with everyone else. On March 23, 1994, when their paths crossed, Tupac punched Allen out as a horrified Albert ran off. Tupac spent ten days in jail.

He got out in time to attend the star-studded premiere of *Above the Rim*. Benjamin Svetkey wrote in *Entertainment Weekly* that "tonight, outside Mann's Chinese Theater on Hollywood Boulevard, Tupac Shakur, 22, is wanted by hundreds of shrieking fans. Crushed against security gates, chanting Two-pack, they watch as the rapper-turned-actor-turned–accused felon arrives via stretch limo at the premiere of *Above the Rim*, in which he plays a killer drug dealer who keeps an amateur hoops team as a hobby. Shakur does not arrive alone. Along with friends and publicists, a sizable chunk of black Hollywood—including Robert Townsend, Patti LaBelle, and members of SWV—has turned out for the occasion."

Once again, Tupac received rave reviews for his performance. *Entertainment Weekly* said,

> As the strong-arm hustler who darts in and out of *Above the Rim*, Tupac Shakur proves, once again, that he may be the most dynamic young actor since Sean Penn. Like Penn, Shakur gives each of his characters a unique spiritual temperature. In *Juice*, he wore a gloomy, reptilian stare—a look of the damned—as the psychotic homeboy who got hooked on murder. Last year, he was an oasis of decency and yearning amid the self-indulgent noise of John Singleton's *Poetic Justice*. Now, he brings barbed comic edges to the role of Birdie, a Harlem operator who carries a razor blade in his mouth and flashes his big, gleaming teeth like a happy wolf.

USA Today reported that Shakur "again comes off as an acting natural." *Rolling Stone* observed that "it's Shakur who steals the show. The rapper's off screen legal problems are well known, but there's no denying his power as an actor."

Meanwhile a political group was making sure that he did not receive the NAACP Image Award for his role in *Poetic Justice*. The National Political Congress of Black Women accused the NAACP of sexism for not withdrawing his nomination as lead actor for *Poetic Justice* after he was arrested on a rape charge. The organization's chairwoman, C. Delores Tucker, accused Tupac of demonstrating "a pattern of behavior that demeaned Black women."

Singer Dionne Warwick said, "Quite frankly, Tupac Shakur is out of control, and so is the NAACP if it does not withdraw his nomination." NAACP spokesman Don Rojas said that withdrawing the nomination would violate the process because Tupac had been nominated before charges were filed against him. He never received the award.

twenty-nine

KEISHA MORRIS

*I*n the chaos that had become Tupac's life, Keisha Morris offered him a sanctuary. A Bronx native, she was a welcome breath of fresh air from the groupies who surrounded Tupac. At their first meeting for a Father's Day dance in the Capitol in New York (formerly Chippendales) club, Keisha instantly recognized him and told her friend Jamie, "Hold my bag. I'm going to dance with Tupac." She strode across the floor, grabbed the rapper, and said, "Come on let's go!"

"We were dancing and he was singing the words to 'C.R.E.A.M.' and I told him, 'That's not your song. Why are you singing that?' He was laughing and then another woman came over. She was trying to get his attention and everything, so I just walked away. I saw him after everyone was partying later on that night and I explained to him, 'You have supporters out here, you know. I know you're going through a difficult time and I wish everything well. I feel you were put in a bad situation.'"

She walked away thinking that she would never see him again but they ran into each other a month later at a club in New York called the Tunnel.

At the time Tupac was staying at the Paramount Hotel. He wanted her to come back there with him but she said, "I'm not going down there."

They debated for an hour until she finally agreed to meet him in the lobby, stressing that she wasn't going up to his room. On that first date, they had "dinner at this little Italian restaurant" and then "went to Chelsea Cinemas in Manhattan to see *Forrest Gump*" the "number one movie in the nation."

After a few more dates, they arranged to meet in Atlanta, where he was to perform at the Vixen in July. Keisha dealt with Tupac's being surrounded by women, understanding that that was "part of the package." Since they'd just met and hadn't invested too much emotion in each other, she felt free to see where events would take them.

She told him, "I'm pretty sure you have a girl in every city. You can't settle down. You're Mr. I Get Around."

But Tupac insisted that he was single and free. "I don't have a girlfriend," going so far as to give her his phone number in Atlanta. Once he did that, she believed him . . . a little.

When she finally saw Tupac's beautiful house, secluded and opulent, it struck Keisha as the bachelor pad that it was. And she could tell from the furniture and accessories that he'd been the one who'd bought it all. But there was more. As Leila Steinberg had discovered years before, Tupac was a slob.

Still there were other things about him that made her love him. He could "throw down" on barbecued chicken. He took her places because he wanted and not because she asked. He loved roller coasters. He started calling her every day, "five times a day."

The relationship took root and "we really started to see each other frequently in September," Keisha recalled. "He went to California. He was out there in the studio for a few days for *Me Against the World* and he came back and bought me another gift."

There were more reasons why she loved him. One was the joy he took in surprising her, like the time he went to her house in New York City while she was still at work:

> He used to make surprise visits to my home all the time. One time I was at work and I didn't expect him to come, but my girlfriend thought he was coming by the things he was saying. But I was like, "I don't think he's coming," because I knew he had some other engagements. When I came home, he was standing in front of my building and about one hundred people were standing in front of my building. He was signing autographs and he said, "I'm gonna kill you." I said, "I'm so sorry." He said, "People went home to get their CDs and tapes. That's how long I've been out here." I said, "Why didn't you tell me?" So we went upstairs and he said, "I have to have the keys." Then he used to come all the time.

Tupac eventually moved in with Keisha. If he'd wanted he could've stayed at his hotel room but he liked a homey atmosphere . . . her homey atmosphere. It was for good reason. They had fun there. They laughed a lot. They got to know each other and shared good memories.

Keisha found it difficult to assess the accuracy of the stories concerning Tupac and the alleged rape. She hadn't known him at the time, and as a woman who appreciated handsome men, she had a hard time believing that someone with Tupac's looks would stoop to such actions. Keisha's desire to be with Tupac as she fell in love with him provided a respite from the looming possibilities that became ever clearer as the trial progressed.

When the trial intruded upon their world, he was living with her in New York. During the trial Keisha was in school but she'd awaken him every morning to make sure that he got dressed and ate. Getting him up was tough since the rapper loved to sleep. But once up, he'd retreat to the bathroom to "write music, write poetry, write anything."

The trial "was every day for about three or four weeks," but Keisha didn't go with him. When Tupac came home, she tried her best to quell the media hype. Home was home and she worked hard to make her space his sanctuary. And while he never showed fear during the trial, he was still bothered by some of the lies being printed about him. Some, like his *Juice* costar Mickey Rourke, showed up to support him, for which he was truly grateful.

Keisha got to see many sides of Tupac and witnessed firsthand the breadth of his creativity and the depths of his quick mind. Always playing in the background, like the grim sounds of a dirge, there was the trial. As it progressed, Tupac spent time with Keisha, basking in the care she showed him. She got his clothes ready, cooked him breakfast, and ensured that he ate well. They joked about Tupac's penchant for writing in the bathroom, but they also argued over his hogging the space.

Time passed. One week became two, then three, and then four. The trial date was approaching fast and the anxiety built. Once it started, Keisha stayed away from the court proceedings. She instead focused on creating an atmosphere that, as much as possible, would shut out the media hype whenever Tupac was home.

But there was only so much Keisha could do. Tupac was sometimes upset from the hearsay being spread about him and his inability to refute the stories. Tupac kept studying his lines. His skill at memorizing so quickly never failed to leave Keisha baffled and impressed with his talent.

As she came to understand, much of Tupac's ability to digest script material so quickly stemmed from his love of the written word. Reading was his passion and Keisha observed quietly as he read material ranging from Marvin Gaye's autobiography to history, literature, and art. They attended the play *Les Miserables*, but she left with the frenetic Tupac before it was over. The man was hungry and even a stage classic couldn't defy his growling stomach.

Keisha had gotten to know Afeni, and Afeni often came up to New York from Atlanta as the trial unfolded. People expected Keisha to bolt when the situation grew tense, but as she'd told Tupac, she was in his corner, not for money, fame, or prestige but for . . . love.

Like other couples, they had their moments of conflict. Keisha was not above demanding to know Tupac's whereabouts and even resorted to rooting through his pockets. Her girlfriends effectively kept tabs on the rapper. For his part, Tupac demanded to know where Keisha was going whenever she went out.

At times, the pressures of the trial overcame Tupac. In November 1994 his frustration with the proceedings came through in his answer to a reporter who was standing outside the courtroom and who simply asked, "How you doin' Tupac?" after the day's proceedings had ended. "Well, I just had to listen to the prosecution's closing argument and it is just so far from the truth that it really has me drained at the end of the day. But I'm leaving it in the hands of the jury. I'm learning a lot about people's innermost fears in this trial. It's not even about my trial anymore. It's about loud, rap music, tattoo-having thugs. It's about some nightmare these people are having. I can't understand why it's this close. They're talking about there is no evidence that I ever sodomized her even though you put that all over the paper. Print the facts so everybody can sort it out. My life is ruined because nobody has a chance to get the facts. . . . There was no semen found . . . no forcible entry . . . no entry into the anal. None of that."

Tupac clearly felt that the media coverage was biased in favor of the prosecution.

Through it all, Keisha and Tupac supported each other. He pushed her to do the best she could in her schoolwork, insisting that she strive for A's rather than settling for B grades. Tupac's energy and love reinforced her own amazing drive as she worked toward a degree in criminal justice and completed an internship with the federal government.

thirty

THE FIRST SHOOTING

What Tupac did next was either desperate, crazy, or a combination of both. He gave an interview to his pal and *New York Daily News* columnist, A. J. Benza. In that interview, he said that Agnant was a "hanger on" and implied that he probably set him up for the rape charge. Tupac was trying to have his cake and eat it too. It had been his decision to hang out in the street with real gangsters and follow the gangster street code. But when trouble came, he pulled his celebrity card and ran to the media.

When the article was published, people who knew the streets shook with fear.

As the trial progressed, the wolves circled ever closer. People talked and much of what they had to say wasn't good. Tupac, frustrated and feeling increasingly isolated (not to mention being tried in a hostile court of public opinion), was anxious to speak out in his own defense. Then he was stunned with news that left him nearly speechless: Jacques "Haitian Jack" Agnant—one of the two men who stayed with Ayanna

Jackson after Tupac left the bedroom on that fateful night—had his case separated from Tupac's and Charles Fuller's.

For a long while things had seemed odd to Tupac. The news of Agnant's move deepened his suspicion. So too did the fact that Agnant's lawyer, Paul Brenner, had done work for the Policemen's Benevolent Association and bragged that "the police are friends of mine."

For someone else, such a boast might've meant nothing. But for Tupac, with his long memory of the government's pursuit of his mother, Mutulu, and other Panther family friends; being harassed by the law himself; and the warnings from Biggie and Iron Mike Tyson, this seemed ominous to Tupac.

Day after day, from November through December 1994, Tupac listened to chief prosecutor Francine James hack away at his life. He and codefendant Charles Fuller were charged with sexual abuse, sodomy, and illegal possession of a firearm.

Tupac's attorney, Michael Warren, countered each onslaught as best he could, but his verbal dexterity couldn't satisfy a public that was in a mood to demand an accounting from rappers, the lifestyles they lived and allegedly promoted, and the grim intersections between fact and rhymed fiction.

While Tupac was tied up in court, his bills, especially the legal kind, were adding up. As he'd said to the reporter, it was nearly impossible to find work. Once the rape charge had been filed against him, Tupac's opportunities to perform dried up. His live shows were canceled and, according to singer Jewell, the rapper's music company, Interscope, had "left him for dead." Royalty checks went straight to the lawyers, and Tupac used his film money to support his family. The brutal poverty of Marin City, Baltimore, and New York seemed closer than it had been in a long while.

For a man of Tupac's colossal pride, being broke and having everyone in the rap industry know it must have been profoundly depleting. Fellow artists invited him to rap on their records for pay and he accepted.

It stank and humiliated him to the nth degree, but he was back to doing what was necessary to survive.

Financial need led Tupac to agree when he got a page from Jimmy Henchman (a.k.a. Booker). The two had been introduced through Agnant, which was troubling to Tupac. But Booker made Tupac an offer. He would pay Tupac to rap on the record of another artist named Lil Shawn, an associate of Biggie Smalls. The link between Booker and Jack was disagreeable, but the link between Biggie and Lil Shawn eased the discomfort. Finally Tupac said, "All right, you give me seven Gs and I'll do the song."

On the way to Quad recording studio, Tupac stopped to get some weed. Booker paged him again, demanding to know, "Where you at? Why ain't you coming?"

"I'm coming, man," Tupac answered. "Hold on."

So Tupac, Randy "Stretch" Walker (who was also good friends with Biggie Smalls), Fred (a friend of Stretch's), and Zane (Sekyiwa's boyfriend) arrived at Quad Studios. A man in army fatigues was standing outside. Tupac rang the bell and was buzzed inside. As they entered the building, the man followed them inside. Two more men in their thirties, also dressed in army fatigues, were sitting in the lobby. They didn't acknowledge him or his entourage. He felt more at ease when Lil Caesar, Biggie's friend from the Junior M.A.F.I.A., hollered down to him from the studio window.

Upon entering the building, Tupac noticed a third man, sitting at a desk and reading a newspaper. He assumed that the other two men and the third one were Biggie's bodyguards, but that didn't explain their failure to acknowledge him.

Part of the confusion was due to the history between Tupac and Biggie. They had collaborated as friends, recording "Runnin" and "House of Pain" together. Tupac had also let Biggie perform in the middle of his concerts when the portly rapper was just starting out. Additionally,

Biggie had stayed with Tupac on visits to L.A. and had gotten some critical advice from Tupac on changing his style to make him more effective on stage and attractive to women. So the coldness from those he thought were Biggie's associates was troubling.

Tupac, Stretch, Freddie, and Zane kept on toward the elevator. Suddenly the three men Tupac had noticed in the lobby pulled out guns and shouted, "Don't nobody move. Everybody on the floor. You know what time it is. Run your shit." Tupac's companions got down on the floor but Tupac did not. "It wasn't like I was being brave or nothing. I just could not get on the floor. They started grabbing at me to see if I was strapped. They said take off your jewels and I wouldn't take them off." One of the men shot Tupac and he went down. The assailants shot him four more times. Tupac lay motionless, hoping that the gunman would think he was dead. "It didn't matter," he later recalled. "They started kicking me, hitting me."

thirty-one

WHAT HAPPENED UPSTAIRS?

Bleeding, Tupac made his way into the elevator. He said that when the door opened and he saw inside the recording studio, "it scared the shit out of me." He claimed that there were at least forty people in the room, including Andre Harrell, Puffy Combs, and Biggie, and that none of them approached him. He called Keisha and told her to alert Afeni. He said that they all seemed surprised to see him even though he had just rung the buzzer downstairs to announce his arrival. All of them were wearing expensive jewelry (why weren't they robbed on their way in?) and everyone just stared at him as he staggered around.

Puffy and Biggie later said that Tupac's story about what happened upstairs was a complete lie. They insisted that everyone showed him love and concern. They remember that he asked for someone to give him a blunt and call his mother. Someone called 911. They say that Tupac never mentioned anyone setting him up. (Note: Puffy [now called Diddy] was the Executive Producer of *Notorious*, the 2009 feature film about Biggie's life. In that film, Tupac [played by Anthony Mackie] does accuse people at the scene of setting him up.) They say that they did

152

everything they could to make him comfortable until the police and ambulance arrived. Months later, the events that did or did not take place upstairs in the recording studio would become very controversial.

What happened next was far scarier. The ambulance showed, followed by the police. "When the cops showed up, Tupac saw some familiar faces. Two of the first four police officers on the scene were William Kelly and Joseph Kelly . . . seconds later, Officer Craig McKernan arrived. McKernan had supervised the two Kellys in Tupac's arrest at the Parker Meridien and had just testified at the rape trial."

What are the odds that a 911 call in a city as large as New York would summon the same three cops who had shown up to help Ayanna Jackson on the day she was attacked and then testified on her behalf in the rape trial?

Paramedics arrived in short order. Tupac's bleeding head was wrapped up and he was placed on a stretcher. By this time, the media was outside Quad. As he was carried out, he realized that a video camera was rolling. He raised a bloody hand and like a true badass, gave the camera the finger. That photo was splashed across the papers and all over TV by morning.

Tupac was rushed into surgery. Hours later, Dr. Leon Pachter, chief of Bellevue Hospital's Trauma Unit, told the press that Tupac "was hit by a low-caliber missile. Had it been a high-caliber missile, he'd be dead."

While lying in his hospital bed, Tupac was shocked to look up and find his mirror image staring back at him. The man was Billy Garland, a New Jersey trucker and former Black Panther who was Tupac's biological father. Garland had not visited Tupac since he was seven years old, when, according to Afeni, "his present to his son was five dollars and a bag of peanuts."

What Tupac and his father talked about is not known. The phone started ringing. Even though Tupac had checked into the hospital under an assumed name, a stranger was getting through. He mentioned coming to the hospital to "finish the job." Tupac checked out of the hospital against the doctor's advice and went to the home of actress Jasmine Guy.

The jury's verdict came the next day, December 1, 1994: not guilty of rape, sodomy, or forcing Jackson to give him oral sex. Specifically, Tupac was convicted of sexual abuse for "forcibly touching the buttocks" of Ayanna Jackson. The *New York Times* called the verdict "ambiguous."

Two months later, he was back in court for sentencing. According to Greg "Shock G" Jacobs, Tupac told the judge, "You know Your Honor throughout this entire court case you haven't looked me or my attorney in the eye once. It is obvious that you're not here in search of justice so therefore there is no point in me asking for a lighter sentence. I don't care what you do because you're not respecting us. This is not a court of law as far as I'm concerned. No justice is being served here and you still can't look me in the eye. So I say do what you want to do. Give me whatever time you want because I'm not in your hands. I'm in God's hands."

Many spectators wiped tears from their eyes.

Judge Fitzgerald was not moved.

Tupac had been in and out of trouble with the law for years. Before handing down the sentence, Judge Fitzgerald told him that ever since he'd become a star, there had been one problem after another. For that reason, he said, he was imposing an eighteen-month to four-and-a-half-year sentence.

Jacques Agnant pled guilty to sexual misconduct and received probation. Charles "Man Man" Fuller received four months in jail.

Tupac spent a few weeks at Riker's Island jail before being transferred to the maximum security Clinton Correctional Facility in Dannemora, New York.

Traumatized Ayanna Jackson later observed that "I admit I did not make the wisest decisions, but I did not deserve to be gang raped."

Tupac believed that Ayanna Jackson was part of a plot to take him down because of the police shootings and the fact that he had such a huge following in the T.H.U.G. L.I.F.E program. With typical candor, he told a *Vibe* reporter that he had nevertheless acted in a cowardly manner in the hotel room. He said that although he did not sexually attack Jackson, he left the room and went to sleep on a couch, making no attempt to protect Ayanna Jackson from the other men because he was afraid that one or more of the men would harm him.

thirty-two

WHERE THE REAL GANGSTAS LIVE

In his December 19, 1995, *New York Times* article "Brutality Behind Bars," Matthew Purdy described the maximum security Clinton Correctional Facility as holding "many of the state's most violent criminals. Most are black and Hispanic men from tough New York neighborhoods. The officers, almost all of them white, are from job-starved Adirondack villages, and many are the sons of guards."

This grim description for the Clinton facility pertained to a prison that opened in 1845 as a wilderness miner's prison. Over one hundred years later, it possessed the reputation of being a tough, no-nonsense institution. For years, New York had sent its worst offenders to the Clinton Correctional Facility, located in a region that had earned the nickname "Little Siberia."

The prison was located near the small town of Dannemora, situated in a deep valley, surrounded by iron mines and the rolling range of hills of Lyon Mountain. Originally built to house only five hundred prisoners, Clinton Correctional steadily grew until it was able to hold over twenty-seven hundred inmates, guaranteeing steady employment to

156

the townsfolk in nearby Dannemora. Their employment opportunities rose and fell in proportion with the miseries inside the prison, and there had been plenty.

During the nineteenth century, there was little concern about how the prisoners at Clinton were treated. They had no bathing facilities, and they were required to wear striped uniforms, spend their days in silence, and walk in lockstep. Some correctional officers made liberal use of leather paddles for disciplining unruly prisoners, occasionally even tying up a prisoner on the floor and beating him. This was a far cry from the idealism that had motivated reformers to overhaul the American prison system during the 1800s.

Prior to 1845, when the Clinton Correctional Facility was built, and especially during the late eighteenth century, long-term imprisonment was not the standard of punishment for offenders. In many cases, criminals were simply executed for being a disturbance to the community; other punishments included whipping, pillorying, and maiming. With such measures available for handling criminals, long imprisonment was perceived as unnecessary and costly. By the late 1700s, more ideas stemming from Europe's period of "enlightenment" found their way into America's collective conscience.

Enlightenment philosophies had been central to the development of liberalized American principles of limited self-government, rights of the individual, and the sanctity of property rights. The impact of those philosophies on society's response to criminals generated a movement away from execution and physical punishment in favor of imprisonment. Since imprisonment in itself did not involve physical harm, it was deemed progressive and humane. In the early decades of the 1800s, however, reformers sought to modify prisons so that those who were incarcerated underwent preparation for a return to society as responsible contributors.

The two states that led the way in overhauling America's prison system, such as it was, were New York and Pennsylvania. Crusaders concerned themselves with not only the means by which prisoners were to be reformed but the physical environment in which they would be rehabilitated. Since such sweeping changes in behavior were unlikely to occur in a short space of time, sentences were lengthened to allow prisoners the opportunity to mend their ways, learn new skills, and become men of industry, responsibility, and temperance.

In Pennsylvania, officials seeking to exact a form of penance from social offenders built penitentiaries. This was consistent with the worldview of the Quakers, who believed that men fell into immorality and depravity as a result of keeping bad company and being exposed to antisocial influences. If kept away from such negative factors in a place where isolation, biblical contemplation, and moderate exercise were the guiding principles of interaction, then they would emerge as better men. New York took a somewhat different route.

New York prison authorities agreed that offenders needed moral reform, but they also believed that keeping prisoners isolated and inactive was cruel and inhuman. Rather than improving an inmate, such treatment would only lead to despair and insanity. A better alternative was to allow prisoners the opportunity to work, learn a skill or trade, grow their own food, make their own clothes, and even produce products for sale to the larger community. From this lofty platform prisoners were supposed to reenter society as not only men of high moral character but equipped with meaningful skills with which to take care of themselves and their families.

The first New York prison based on this revised philosophy opened in Auburn in 1819. By the time the Clinton Correctional Facility opened in 1845, the Auburn system of prison construction, function, and rehabilitation had evolved to a point of satisfaction for most officials. The new methodology offered a system that ran a prison with industrial efficiency while also producing revenues from product sales that mitigated the costs of the institution's operation.

But local craftsmen and artisans in nearby Dannemora did not view the competition with prison labor in a positive light. From their vantage point, having to compete with prison labor was unfair and they voiced their protests to local and state officials. Legislators hesitated to lose the benefits of a burgeoning prison industrial enterprise and placated locals with promises to limit the amount of work prisoners performed. Most often, officials simply silenced the voices of concern rather than resolve the stated problem.

As the Clinton facility grew, violence inside the prison also became more commonplace. By 1870, the Auburn system had produced prisons throughout the country that, rather than having rehabilitation as their main objective, were dedicated to warehousing society's most troublesome characters in maximum security detention.

The severity of conditions drew the ire of a new generation of reformers who at the 1870 founding meeting of the National Prison Association collectively reminded prison officials that the goal of incarceration was reformation, not the "vindictive suffering" of the inmates. Their protests fell on mostly deaf ears, and conditions at facilities like Clinton worsened.

In July 1929, sixteen hundred Clinton inmates rioted due to the overcrowded conditions. The state responded swiftly and three prisoners were killed in the effort to restore order. In subsequent years, the conditions inside Clinton and the atmosphere of violence grew worse. Outbreaks of violence resulted in the deaths of numerous prison guards. Acts of arson were common, and guards subjected prisoners to increasing brutality.

In the twentieth century, Clinton Correctional Facility's reputation as a place of misery and brutality was underscored by the infamy of the convicts who were imprisoned there. In the 1940s, lethal mobster and father of modern organized crime, Salvatore Lucania (a.k.a. Lucky Luciano), who had run crime operations throughout the United States was sentenced to thirty to fifty years. Although Luciano had been involved with bookmaking, extortion, loan-sharking, and murder, he was prosecuted for allegedly running a prostitution ring.

Another Clinton inmate was David Berkowitz (a.k.a. Son of Sam). In the late 1970s, Berkowitz terrorized New York City during a killing spree in which he murdered six people and wounded seven others. Berkowitz was sentenced to 365 years in Attica and was later transferred to the Clinton facility; he was subsequently transferred to the truly miserable facility at Attica.

In the late 1980s, Robert E. Chambers Jr. (a.k.a. the Preppie Killer) was sentenced to fifteen years in prison for the brutal sex slaying of eighteen-year-old Jennifer Levin. Chambers, a tall, handsome man, was a miscreant who'd been kicked out of Boston College for theft and eventually entangled himself in burglaries, alcoholism, and drug abuse. Early on August 26, 1986, Chambers murdered Levin. He denied any involvement but discounted his own story when authorities were given a tape of him at a party, laughing and joking, as he pretended to enact the crime. Chambers was sent to Auburn State Prison and eventually moved to the Clinton facility. He served more time when heroin was found in his cell and new charges were brought.

With such unsavory inhabitants in Clinton Correctional Facility, the guards having charge over them could not afford to be shrinking violets. Nonetheless, excessive behavior by guards commanded the scrutinizing attention of the press and public.

On June 29, 1987, the Associated Press reported that a prisoner had been shot by a guard, and four others suffered knife wounds, during a disturbance that broke out in the exercise yard. The following year, on July 10, 1988, Isabel Wilkerson of the *New York Times* reported on the events surrounding the injuries sustained by eleven guards and eight prisoners from a clash in the facility. In 1995, two Clinton guards were ordered to pay over $14,000 for viciously assaulting an inmate. This was but the tip of the iceberg of the hostile environment inside the prison.

The violence between prisoners and guards was an oblique reflection of the hostility and violence that most likely existed throughout the Clinton facility. The humane objectives of nineteenth-century reformers for such prisons by the time Tupac Shakur arrived there had long been supplanted by expediency, cruelty, terror, and ubiquitous violence.

thirty-three

ME AGAINST THE WORLD

On April 1, 1995, Interscope released *Me Against the World*. Its overall tone was somber. Recorded after the shooting at Quad Studios, it not surprisingly dealt with pain, fatigue, isolation, fear, and death. "Dear Mama" suggested that Tupac had always held Afeni in high regard even when she was a hard-core crack addict. Afeni says, " . . . Tupac asked me if I was using drugs and I told him I was smoking, but I had it under control. I told them that there was no problem. And my son believed me. And that's why he didn't forgive me, because I lied. Basically that's what it was for him. He never got past that I lied. . . . "

However, Tupac did not record "Dear Mama" just for himself. He knew that there were thousands of young men and women like him who had suffered through the misery of living with a drug-addicted parent. He was right. It became one of his biggest hits and is considered one of the greatest rap songs ever made.

In the bleak tune "Me Against the World" the male protagonist finds himself watching his friends and neighbors get murdered and carted off to the cemetery. No one cares about him, he is broke and almost insane from worrying about what will become of him although he wishes that he were rich and had the political clout to change the fortunes of the people who live around him.

"So Many Tears" was another hit from the album and Tupac is clearly rapping about himself. He talks about his childhood when he just needed peace of mind and how he didn't feel right until the words T.H.U.G. L.I.F.E. were emblazoned across his chest. He has cried for so long about so many things that he is tired of living and wishes for an early death to take away the pain.

It debuted at number one on the Billboard charts, beating Bruce Springsteen, and it showcased Tupac at his raw and emotionally heart-rending best. One reviewer called *Me Against the World* "a remarkable and insightful musical achievement which created a flow of inspiration and vibes through all who heard it."

Tupac remains the first and only musician to have the number one album in the country while doing time in jail.

thirty-four

THE SHOGUN OF DEATH ROW

𝕴n later years, some would wonder how Marion "Suge" Knight ended up ruling a musical empire that inspired both amazement and loathing. But in the early 1990s, the general public could be forgiven for failing to discern that an organization calling itself Death Row Records was destined to be a major innovative powerhouse in the music industry.

Ironically, Suge Knight's disposition as a child had been so sweet and adorable that his father, Marion, had nicknamed him "Sugar Bear." But by the 1990s, the once adorable "Sugar Bear" had grown into a massive 6-foot-3, 330-pound presence, resembling a bear in size only; all traces of the sugar were long gone.

Marion "Suge" Knight Jr. was born on April 19, 1964, into a blue-collar family. His father, Marion Sr., worked in the facilities department at UCLA and his mother, Maxine, worked on the assembly line at an electronics manufacturer. In 1969, after nine years of marriage, they bought a gray stucco one-story home with two bedrooms, one bath, barred windows, and a tiny front lawn in the working-class suburb of Compton.

The Knight household, which included two other children, both girls, provided a sense of security and warmth that suited their young son's sweet disposition. However, the streets beyond the front door of their Compton home were far from inviting. By the mid-1960s, Compton, a city of predominately racially mixed people, was experiencing changes that eventually resulted in the loss of manufacturing jobs in the area and the rise of two of the most ruthless street gangs in American history: the Bloods and Crips.

A branch of the Bloods known as the Leudis Park Piru Bloods operated close to Suge's home, but he managed to escape their influence. By the time he was a teenager Suge had become immersed in the far "safer" world of competitive football. Even so, the desire to fit in and not be seen as soft and vulnerable moved Suge to establish friendships with some Bloods even as he excelled in football.

His reputation for hard, bone-jarring play on the gridiron and his towering size combined to win him letters in both track and football at Lynwood High School and a football scholarship to El Camino Community College after his high school graduation in 1983. The following year, Suge attracted the attention of a football recruiter from the University of Nevada–Las Vegas and was admitted to the school.

Some teammates gossiped about Suge's alleged connection to the Bloods, causing school administrators to worry, but Suge eventually won them over. In subsequent weeks and months, his hard work, determination, and discipline won their full confidence and he was named rookie of the year.

During the off-season, Suge earned money as a bouncer at nightspots like the Cotton Club and West Side Story and enjoyed the music coming from East Coast rappers like Run-DMC, the Fat Boys, Big Daddy Kane, and EPMD.

In 1987, during Suge's senior year with UNLV, he left school to play football with the Los Angeles Rams as a reserve lineman. He was called up to fill in for regular players who were on strike and was dropped from the roster once the strike ended. This blow to his professional aspirations was mirrored in his personal life when longtime girlfriend Sharitha Golden broke off their relationship.

Suge didn't take the news well and Golden eventually took out a restraining order against him to protect herself, her mother, her sister, and her aunt, all of whom had been urging her to dump Suge. He was unfazed.

In a later altercation, he threatened to tow her car away and then assaulted her. It was an early glimpse of a bad temper. On another occasion he tried to steal a car, which got him charged with attempted murder, grand larceny/auto, and use of a deadly weapon. Somehow the charges were reduced to two misdemeanors. Suge pleaded guilty and was fined $1,000. This wouldn't be his last run-in with the law.

He and Sharitha reconciled and eventually got married.

Suge eventually found work as a bodyguard for musicians. The 1980s were hurtling toward their end and rap music and hip-hop culture were moving westward, blazing a trail of new sounds, traditions, perspectives, and reactions.

New York had given birth to hip-hop but it was the L.A. scene that soon caught the nation's attention. It wasn't the first time, and surely wouldn't be the last, that East Coast and West Coast vied for prominence in the ever-changing world of pop culture.

As early as the 1970s, break dancing (i.e., breaking), while being refined in New York, had been further shaped by dance styles referred to as locking and popping. These were upright dances in which the dancers used their arms, legs, and torsos in isolated semirobotic moves requiring great body control.

Everything changed in 1989 when N.W.A. released *Straight Outta Compton*. While the group referred to its music as "reality rap," the media quickly dubbed it gangsta rap and the name stuck. The effects were thunderous. N.W.A. and the success it generated unleashed "the dark imaginations of young black artists, freeing them to use raw language to say things on vinyl no generation of African Americans had felt comfortable expressing in public."

Suge was not interested in becoming a performer nor did he want to continue guarding them. He wanted a record company of his own. He struck paydirt when he landed a gig working with the D.O.C. (real name Tracy Lynn Curry), a talented rapper who was the protégé of Andre "Dr. Dre" Young, a gifted record producer and member of N.W.A. As Suge listened to the D.O.C. talk about the problems that N.W.A. were having, it sounded to him like the talent over at Ruthless Records was being undercompensated. The D.O.C. eventually introduced Suge to Dr. Dre, who decided to become his partner and establish a new record company. This was easier said than done. There are many lurid tales about how Suge got Eric "Eazy-E" Wright to release Dr. Dre from his contract.

One spellbinding story (sounding like a scene from *The Godfather*) had Suge confronting Eazy-E with bats and pipes and threatening to harm his mother if he didn't sign the release form.

What's beyond dispute is that Eazy-E filed a lawsuit against Death Row Records, Dr. Dre, Suge, and others for making him sign the release under duress. The racketeering charges were dismissed but the courts did decide that Dr. Dre would have to pay a certain amount of his earnings to Ruthless Records until the term of the contract was up.

Free to move forward, Suge and Dr. Dre began to build a stable of artists. The assemblage of rappers who eventually comprised the collection of stars in Death Row's glittering constellation of talent included some of the most colorful, hard-working, creative, and determined young people in the music industry.

SNOOP DOGG

Like a music story straight out of 1960s Motown, Cordazar Calvin Broadus (a.k.a. Snoop Doggy Dogg) gained his early music experience by singing in church. His name stemmed from the nickname his mother gave him as a child due to the way he dressed and his love for the comic strip *Peanuts*.

Born October 20, 1972, in Long Beach, California, on the outskirts of Compton, Snoop grew up to be a tall, scrawny kid with a sharp chin and protruding cheekbones. He could at times be vulnerable but at other times gave the appearance of being quite dangerous. The dangerous side wasn't all show, as evidenced by his eventual membership in the Rolling 20 street gang, a branch of the infamous Crips.

One of three boys being raised by his single mother, Snoop collected rap records and aspired to make it in the rap game. When he discovered that his friends were making more money on the streets than he was on his after-school job, he joined them in the streets. Once he joined the Rolling 20 Crips in Long Beach, he started selling crack cocaine but never lost his love for rap, penning lyrics and practicing in his spare time. It was the 1980s, and the New York rap scene still dominated. Snoop loved the skillful storytelling of the rapper Slick Rick.

Meanwhile Snoop's stint as a crack dealer resulted in a series of unpleasant stays behind bars. During one stint, older, wiser inmates heard his lyrics and said: "Young nigga, you need to be out there rapping, getting paid." The message got through, and after his last release (and determining that making money was better than wasting time in jail), Snoop returned to Long Beach and got to work on his music.

Snoop, Nathaniel Hale (a.k.a. Nate Dogg), and Warren Griffin (a.k.a. Warren G), the stepbrother of Death Row cofounder Donald Smith (a.k.a. Lil ½ Dead), formed the group 213 (in recognition of a local telephone area code).

The hopeful artists of 213 spent the early months of 1991 trying to get an audience with Dr. Dre by having Warren G take samples of their recordings to him. Dre wasn't impressed and 213's future looked bleak. They were persistent, however, and Dre eventually listened to their music during a stag party at his house.

The music clicked and Dre sent word that he wanted to meet with Snoop. Dre had been looking for a song for his upcoming *Deep Cover* album. It was Snoop's big chance to impress the Doctor. He did.

Over the next few years, Snoop was the subject of both fame and infamy. He contributed heavily to Dre's 1992 debut album, *The Chronic*. There is no overstating the impact that *The Chronic*, which sold over 3 million copies, had on the rap music industry. Before *The Chronic*, performers had a choice about whether to do political, party, comedy, gangsta, or sexy rap. After *The Chronic*, gangsta rap practically became the industry standard and it was hard to get a record deal or huge promotional dollars if you were doing anything else. A lot of hits came off that album—"Nuthin but a G Thang," "Fuck wit Dre Day," "Let Me Ride"—and most rap music aficionados consider it one of the best rap albums in the history of the genre.

Snoop's vocals on *The Chronic* gave him the exposure he needed for his 1993 release of *Doggystyle*, which sold more copies in its opening week than the rest of the top five combined, the highest number ever for a debut album.

Then tragedy struck. On August 25, 1993, Snoop and his bodyguard, McKinley Lee, were riding around in the Woodbine Park section of L.A. when they pulled over to talk with some men in a park. They'd seen one of the men earlier, arguing with one of Snoop's friends. Then twenty-year-old Ethiopian immigrant Philip Woldemariam approached Snoop's Jeep and pulled a gun. Lee pulled his weapon and shot Woldemariam twice; he later died. Snoop and Lee found themselves in the eye of a legal storm but were eventually acquitted when a jury found them not guilty on the basis of self-defense.

WARREN GRIFFIN

Warren Griffin (a.k.a. Warren G) had the phenomenal luck of his father having been married to Dr. Dre's mother, Verna. This made them stepbrothers and therefore family. His group, 213, broke up without ever making a record. Warren G was never actually signed to Death Row but he did a significant amount of work on *The Chronic* and many other Death Row records. In 1993, Warren G produced the track "Indo Smoke" featuring himself, Nate Dogg, and Mista Grimm.

When Warren sought a deal of his own, Dre replied, "You need to go and be your own man." Translation: no deal was forthcoming. The slight did not go down well with Warren but he had no choice but to take his talent elsewhere—Def Jam Records. Warren scored a hit with his 1994 Def Jam debut *Regulate . . . The G-Funk Era*, but his next effort, *Take a Look over Your Shoulder*, was less successful.

Warren's stunted career did not leave him without some degree of bitterness. In an interview with *The Source* his bile spilled out when he claimed that "I made Death Row." He quickly retracted the statement, but it was too late. Once the word got out, Warren awakened one night to see guns in his face and was ordered to never let such words escape his lips again.

KURUPT

Kurupt (a.k.a. Ricardo Brown), from Philadelphia, wanted to be a smooth operator with women, like his rapping heroes, Spoonie Gee and Rakim. His teenage rebelliousness forced his mother to ship him to California to live with his father. On the West Coast, he pursued his rapping dream and one night wound up in a rap battle with Snoop Dogg.

The two competitors felt a strong sense of camaraderie and agreed that if one or the other got a record deal, then the one who'd had such good fortune would look out for his friend. So when Snoop Dogg got his deal with Death Row, Kurupt was also signed. The combination of Kurupt and Snoop's cousin, Delmar Drew Arnaud (a.k.a. Daz Dillinger, a.k.a. Dat Nigga Daz) formed the Dogg Pound. They made their debut in 1992 on Dr. Dre's production of *The Chronic* and Snoop's controversial 1993 *Doggystyle*.

LADY OF RAGE

No one could ever accuse Robin Evette Allen of not being able to compete with the guys. At 175 pounds and sporting a 1970s Afro puff hairstyle, Allen had come to the attention of Dr. Dre by way of a group called the L.A. Posse, "a group of producers that hailed from the West Coast and had produced the majority of LL Cool J's second album, *Bigger and Deffer*." The meeting had been a long time coming.

Born in Virginia but raised mostly in Texas, Allen tried several times to commit suicide while growing up. Perhaps she was attempting to escape from the tight moral strictures of her mother and grandfather. By adulthood she possessed a wild streak and a generous dose of adventurism. The latter quality propelled her to New York by way of Arkansas.

She managed to appear on a record for L.A. Posse, but nothing happened for her after that. She was left homeless and hanging out in lower Manhattan's Chun King Studios. And that's where Dre, seeking to add to his and Suge Knight's growing list of talent at Death Row, found Allen. She delivered a hit single called "Afro Puffs" but spent most of her time on collaborations with other Death Row artists like Snoop Dogg.

From the moment Tupac became a part of Death Row, he was all about business. The pace he set for himself astounded even veteran workaholics like Dr. Dre. One day Dr. Dre had Tupac listen to the beats for a song he called "California Love." "So what do you think?" Dre asked, going on to inquire whether or not Tupac needed another listen before he could write some lyrics.

Tupac wasn't bothered. "I'm ready to go right now," he answered. "Let's do it." He made up lyrics to go with the beats right on the spot. Dre was astounded. "That's some incredible shit," he commented to a friend.

"California Love," which features Dr. Dre, was Tupac's comeback dance single and a remarkable song. It celebrates California as a place to live, party, and have a good time. Dr. Dre kicks it off with the line "I wanna welcome everybody to the Wild Wild West." He goes on to rap about his career in the "sunshine state . . . where ya never find a dance floor empty." Then Tupac jumps in and rocks it to "serenade the streets of L.A. from Oakland to Sacktown, the Bay Area, and back down" until it is impossible for the listener to sit still. You simply have to get up and dance.

Tupac also thought he'd get a chance to work with his longtime friend and confidante from his days back in Baltimore, Jada Pinkett. She wanted to direct the "California Love" music video and had been meeting with Dr. Dre about it. But then she took herself off the project. It didn't take long to figure out why.

Will Smith was Jada's boyfriend and he had no great love for gangsta rap. But more than that, Will knew of the link between his wife and Tupac. They were close friends and he wasn't about to give a lame nod to a circumstance that would've allowed them to get closer. So Jada was off the project. It went forward with Jada's Mad Max concept anyway.

It reached number one on the Billboard Hot 100, was nominated at the Grammy Awards for Best Rap Solo Performance as well as Best Rap

Performance by a Duo or Group. It eventually was ranked number 346 on *Rolling Stone* magazine's 500 greatest songs of all time.

Before the bright, promising vision of a black-owned and operated record industry powerhouse turned into a nightmare of envy, intrigue, and pain, Marion "Suge" Knight's Death Row Records defied odds and expectations, ruled the airwaves as the heart and soul of hip-hop, and scored stratospheric sales figures that silenced the skeptics.

To the outside world, Death Row was filled with overgrown delin-quents bent on causing mischief and determined to invite America's young people to join in the mayhem. But in the early days Death Row had provided a refuge for artists who had been rejected by society, con-fined to urban armpits of poverty and despair, daily assaulted by insti-tutions robbing black children of their dignity and dreams, and were deemed suspects by law enforcement as soon as they stepped into the streets.

The tunes were rapped by artists who themselves had had rude brushes with the law. They were rough around the edges but boiling over with talent. They were young in years but hard times had made them old in spirit. They were unschooled in the niceties of gently com-municating their message since life hadn't often been nice or gentle with them. They were tired of running into walls erected by hands they couldn't see, and rapping was their ladder to freedom. They'd been told repeatedly that failure was their destiny but success lived in their spirits. Television put opulence within their sight, but despair was all they were able to grasp. Trouble for the nation was brewing in the urban hinter-lands and these artists knocked on America's door with rapped warn-ings that somebody had better wake up. Knight had no formal business education and didn't work his way up the music industry ladder. This worked in his favor. It freed him to think outside the box and create in-novative marketing plans. He wasn't polished enough to socialize with corporate types, and so he avoided socializing with them. Rather than playing golf or pool with other music executives, Knight focused on building the company. Death Row was for the artists. It was their home; it was their refuge; it was their relief. If they were rejected by everyone and everything else, they'd always be accepted there.

Unlike organizations that viewed artists as replaceable commodities with limited shelf life, Suge believed that his rappers were central to Death Row operations. Without them there was no company, and he tried to keep them engaged, paid, satisfied, and happy. He assured them that they mattered not just as performers but as human beings.

Basic respect was something many of them had never experienced. They knew about being abandoned. They knew about having to fight for survival. At Death Row, they could relax. They felt that Suge would never abandon them.

Suge Knight got stellar performances from Death Row stars for the fundamental reason that they believed he really loved them. Their certainty that he was genuinely interested in them and their well-being was reciprocated. Suge had to make money. If they got famous, Suge deserved to share that glory. If Death Row was his baby, then it was their child too.

As a result, Death Row skyrocketed into being a place where artists couldn't wait to work. Other record companies now came looking for Suge to divine the Death Row secret. Music industry execs who just a short time before wouldn't have given Suge the time of day now had to wait their turn to share a few quick moments with the genius behind the phenomenally successful Death Row Records.

"The most important thing about business is being real to the community and being real to the streets," Suge declared. "The talent comes from the streets, not the [business] suites."

This was sweet comfort for people who'd spent most of their lives unsure about whether or not even family members would be there for them in time of need. Suge gave them that guarantee. They understood that if they suffered, he'd suffer with them. If they profited, he'd celebrate their wealth. And he'd never, ever take the credit. Suge Knight's method of running operations at Death Row was based on trust, loyalty, harmony, joy, and love. Where other people ran a business, he ran a "family." But all had a place and they were expected to fulfill their assigned roles. Just as Suge had no intention of hogging center stage with the artists, he didn't brook any interference in the running of the business. Decisions on when to release a record, or not, were made by him. Keeping the peace and good relations was expected of all and enforced by him. It was all in the interests of keeping the Death Row family strong.

thirty-five

INMATE NO. 95-A-1140

After the shooting at Quad, Tupac recuperated in the New York apartment of actress Jasmine Guy. Afeni hovered over his bed and waited on him hand and foot. He appeared to enjoy ordering her around and watching her clean, cook, and fetch for him as she had not done for him and Sekyiwa when they were younger. By the time Tupac went to prison, Afeni had been clean for at least three years. She was his biggest supporter while he was locked up, and it was during that terrible eleven-month span when he was in Dannemora that mother and son were able to mend their broken hearts and love each other fully again.

Angela Ardis, a gorgeous young woman who lived in Atlanta, Georgia, where she worked as a marketing assistant and part-time model, started writing to Tupac while he was being held on Riker's Island. They became friends and continued exchanging letters and poems after he was locked down at Clinton Correctional Facility. In their writings, they revealed their life stories and hopes for the future. But before dreams of the future could be indulged, Tupac, also known as Inmate no. 95-A-1140, had to get through every agonizing moment of his present.

Because of his celebrity, prison officials tried to place Tupac in the protective custody unit. Tupac refused. Angela thought that "it was important for Tupac to feel as if he was as hard and respected as 'he' thought he was. I believe that at times, he believed his own hype. To refuse protective custody, meant that he lived by his words and the men inside related to him as much as he related to himself. In believing that, he probably felt as if he had nothing to fear. Like he always said, 'I fear no man but God.'"

He told her that he was born on June 16, 1971, to Afeni Shakur and Kenneth Saunders (Legs). He knew by then that Billy Garland, the man who had come to see him in the hospital, was his biological father. Was this just wishful thinking? Angela says, "Maybe Tupac felt closer to Kenneth Saunders than he did his biological father. We all know that biological does not make you a father but the time and respect put in makes one feel as though that person deserves the title. To Tupac, Kenneth Saunders may have put in the work, hence, was rewarded with the title."

He also told Angela that Afeni couldn't keep a man because she was strong and dominating and, when he left Baltimore for Marin City, all Afeni had to give him was her last five dollars and four chicken wings to eat on the bus. Unfortunately, Afeni's boyfriend had recently assaulted her, so Tupac had to ride all the way to California with the image of his mother's black eye in mind.

Tupac's letters also revealed a conscientious young man who supported a large extended family at a very young age: "I financially take care of my mother, aunt, uncle, female cousin Jamala, sista Sekyiwa. Cousins: Malcolm, Dena, Nelson, Helena, Bill, Kenny and many others 2 many to name." According to those who knew him, a lot of this support continued until the day he died. Angela Ardis's memoir, *Inside a Thug's Heart,* contains all of the letters that she and Tupac exchanged during his incarceration.

Not surprisingly, Tupac had a tough time adjusting to prison life but he avoided weighing people down with his troubles.

Tupac married Keisha Morris on April 29, 1995. Once he had a wife, Tupac had someone he could trust to handle his business dealings. He also had a reason to stay alive inside his prison hellhole.

From the start of his incarceration nightmare, Tupac wrote to keep Keisha informed of his whereabouts and activities. She called daily, doing her part to stay informed about the location and condition of her heart. She gave her all, working every day to make money to get Tupac whatever he needed. Keisha's work ethic, imprinted by her hardworking parents, was on full display in Tupac's time of need.

Keisha eventually altered her life to spend as much time as possible near Tupac once he started serving his sentence at Dannemora. He was always glad to see her. She brought him what he needed. Then they got married. They'd talked about it before, and it was an idea that appealed to Keisha. Tupac called her his queen and she looked upon him as her king. But Keisha was more than a queen: she was a saint.

She took an apartment in town near the prison and did her best to provide Tupac with the material and emotional support that could ease the difficulties of his predicament. Even under those horrid conditions she sought to make the marriage work, but the confinement was getting to Tupac. Keisha could only guess, and didn't really want to know, the gritty details of what her husband was enduring behind bars.

Tupac's frustration grew into rage. He displaced his anger onto Keisha, and it hurt. She'd been there for him. She'd changed her life, sacrificed her sweat and treasure to meet his needs. She understood that the Tupac lashing out at her was an ugly facsimile of the man she'd known. But that man had been free and easygoing. That man hadn't lived in a cage. That man could have barely guessed what awaited him behind prison walls.

Kevin Powell, a reporter for *Vibe*, had interviewed Tupac at Riker's Island. His article finally appeared in the magazine's April 1995 issue and the matter of what really happened the night he was shot at the Quad Recording Studio became hotly debated once again. Tupac had used the street names of many people who were mentioned in the article, which exposed them to police scrutiny.

Stretch was furious because Tupac seemed to criticize him for hitting the floor so fast and not resisting the bandits. "I ain't dumb. I ain't got no gun, what the fuck am I supposed to do?"

It seemed like everyone who'd been at Quad that night became bitter and angry after reading what Tupac had to say. They contacted *Vibe* to rebut his story and some of their comments were printed in a future issue. All of them said that when a bloody Tupac got off the elevator, they rushed to help him.

Andre Harrell added that when the paramedics arrived he told Stretch to ride in the ambulance with Tupac "cause I wasn't trusting the police with Tupac. He had too many open issues with the police. I was feeling like something could have happened between the ride and the hospital."

Biggie said, "When I read the interview, I felt like he was shitting on everybody." Puffy stated, "I hope that his Thug Life shit is really over. But on the real, if you gonna be a motherfuckin' thug, you gots to live and die a thug . . . There ain't no jumpin in and out of thuggism."

Stretch felt the same way: "Why would he go and do an interview like that? He's supposed to be a street nigga; he should've kept it in the street . . . niggas had to go and get their name changed . . . I want him to get a reality check."

The East Coast/West Coast war was about to start but neither Tupac nor Biggie started it. The first shot was fired while Tupac was still in prison.

In August 1995 during the Source Hip-Hop Music Awards in Madison Square Garden, Suge Knight took the stage and said, "Any artist out there who wants to be an artist and stay a star, and don't wanna have to worry about the executive producer trying to be all in the videos, all on the records, dancing . . . come to Death Row."

It was a clear swipe at Puffy Combs and people in the audience started to boo. After all, the event was taking place on the East Coast where Puffy and Biggie were admired.

Snoop Dogg was angered by the booing. He took the stage and confronted the audience: "The East Coast ain't got no love for Dr. Dre and Snoop Dogg and Death Row?" he asked. "Y'all don't love us?" He repeated the question again, "Y'all don't love us?" When the audience didn't react the way he wanted it to, he shouted "We know y'all East Coast . . . We know where the fuck we at . . . So let it be known then!"

The media ran with the story. Over the next twelve months reporters interviewed and reinterviewed every rapper they could find, repeating even minor insults. They sold plenty of newspapers and magazines by reporting on (some critics say, creating) what they dubbed the war between East Coast and West Coast.

A few weeks later, Quincy Jones held a summit to talk about the state of hip-hop. The meeting was held in New York and the speakers included Ed Lewis from *Essence*, Colin Powell, Fab 5 Freddy as moderator, and Malcolm X's eldest daughter, Attalah Shabazz.

The attendees included John Singleton, Dr. Dre, Suge Knight, Chuck D, Puffy Combs, Andre Harrell, Keith Clinkscales from *Vibe*, Jermaine Dupri, and Biggie Smalls. The speakers told the rap contingent that "the anger unleashed by hip-hop had to be dealt with and steered in a more positive direction."

Speaker after speaker talked about power as a form of responsibility, about talent as a power that shouldn't be used to destroy, and "about being guided by the inner conscience." Three weeks later, one of Suge

Knight's closest friends, Jake Robles, was shot to death in Atlanta after a birthday party. A witness said that Puffy's bodyguard fired the shot. A grief-stricken Suge Knight angrily blamed Puffy for his murder.

Miles away in the grim surroundings of his new home, Tupac dealt with more immediate problems. The guards were giving him a hard time. He'd been placed on twenty-three-hour lockdown for smoking marijuana, and he was wary of lifers who had nothing to lose by killing someone.

He put feelers out on the street to find out who was behind the shooting at Quad. His informants (whom he never named) reported that Biggie and Puffy had at the very least known about the ambush and did not warn him. Tupac was shocked, hurt, and angry. He and Biggie had been friends after the Quad shooting. In fact, Tupac hadn't been angry with Puffy either. When Puffy volunteered to come to the prison and sit down and talk to him about the situation, Tupac had said it wasn't necessary. But he understandably pressed a lot of people for answers about what really happened that night, and the responses he got enraged him.

Tupac had been talking about getting out of the rap business and concentrating on making movies. But when he received the news, it shook him to the core: "I'm going to make them sorry that they ever did this to me," he vowed.

Speaking about Biggie, he said in a prison interview, "Fear is stronger than love . . . all the love that I gave out didn't mean nothing when it came to fear." In other words, friends would only remain friends until someone scarier came along and then they would align themselves with the scary person.

Suge Knight made several visits to the prison, and it was clear that the two men were planning something. Over the years, Suge Knight had repeatedly asked Tupac to sign with Death Row Records, but Tupac had always turned him down. Now things were different. He told Keisha to contact the mogul. If Suge could raise the bail money to get him out of prison, then he'd join the Death Row roster.

Many wondered why Tupac had aligned himself with Suge Knight who, though a brilliant marketer, was reputedly involved in violent and criminal activity. But there weren't any other wealthy or influential people trying to get him out of the maximum-security penitentiary.

Tupac had powerful enemies whom he feared. Knight's reputation (justified or not) suggested that he could handle anything or anybody that came his way. In addition, Tupac had received word that there was a possible jail contract out on him. If that was true, the only way he'd leave the prison was in a box. He desperately needed money and freedom.

Suge and his attorney, David Kenner, pulled it together: Suge would put up $250,000 of the $1.4 million that it would take to spring Tupac. Interscope and MCA would chip in the rest. Cheo Hodari Coker wrote that "it was just as Tupac had learned in his childhood; revolutionaries had rhetoric but gangsters made things happen."

On a crisp autumn morning in October 1995, a white stretch limousine pulled up outside the prison gates. Tupac got in and the car rolled away. There was a private jet waiting to fly Tupac to Los Angeles.

part four

AVENGER

thirty-six

THE MAN WHO WALKED
OUT OF PRISON

B ack when he was in the Riker's Island city jail, Tupac told *Vibe* reporter Kevin Powell, "I was letting people dictate who should be my friends. I felt like because I was this big Black Panther type of nigga, I couldn't be friends with Madonna. And so I dissed her, even though she showed me nothing but love. I felt bad, because when I went to jail, I called her and she was the only person that was willing to help me. Of that stature. Same thing with Mickey Rourke—he just befriended me. Not like black and white, just like friend to friend. And, from now on, it's not going to be a strictly black thing with me."

But first there was a score to settle.

Before Tupac was sent to Riker's Island and then to Clinton Correctional Facility, he loved the dispossessed, the poverty stricken, and anyone who felt hopeless. He spent a lot of time sympathizing with young people who lived in dysfunctional homes with addicted parents and young people who lived in foster or group homes. He hurt for grownups who had been hurt as children. Many of his song lyrics were filled with such personal angst that they read like pages from a diary. Those who listened to the words could sense his pain and understood that he felt theirs too.

Proof of Tupac's connection with those on the margins was found in heart-rending songs like "Brenda's Got a Baby," "Hear Me, Keep Ya Head Up," and "Dear Mama." He had once been one of them and he never forgot that.

The man who walked out of prison still loved hopeless people, but they were no longer his obsession. He had two new ones: proving that he could rise once more to the pinnacle of rap music success and getting even with Biggie, the former friend who, he felt, had betrayed him.

He was now a convicted sex offender and the label grated at him in a way his friends say was frightening to witness. Those who knew him before he was shot and imprisoned say that on the outside, he appeared to be the same old Tupac. But the idealism of his earlier years had shriveled into a bitter remnant of itself. If one listened closely, traces of it could still be heard, but very rarely.

Tupac reveled in returning home to sunny California. After giving some interviews and taking care of personal errands, he headed for Can Am Studios and got to work.

By all outward appearances he seemed to be the same old Pac, but inside he felt abandoned by many artists who hadn't come to visit him in jail.

As for Keisha, she felt that he was far from ready to be a real husband and filed for a marriage annulment. Once again, Tupac was navigating life on his own.

A few weeks after his release, Tupac was interviewed by *Los Angeles Times* staff writer Chuck Phillips. He told Phillips, "I'm so glad to be out. It was tough sitting in jail listening to Jay Leno and Rush Limbaugh and everybody making jokes about me getting shot. It's been stress and drama for a long time now, man. So much has happened. I got shot five times by some dudes who were trying to rub me out. But God is great. He let me come back. But when I look at the last few years, it's not like everybody did me wrong. I made some mistakes. But I'm ready to move on."

Instead of asking Tupac why "some dudes" were trying to "rub him out," Phillips just wanted to know how Tupac felt about so many people perceiving his music as a glorification of criminal activity and violence. Tupac had answered questions like these many times over the years. There was no new ground to be covered here. Wearily, he tried one more time to explain his music. "Let me say for the record, I am not a gangster and never have been. I'm not the thief who grabs your purse. I'm not the guy who jacks your car. I'm not down with people who steal and hurt others. I'm a brother who fights back. I'm not some violent closet psycho. I've got a job. I'm an artist."

Tupac told Chuck Phillips that he was "ready to move on," but it wasn't long before he publicly accused Biggie of copying his style. Some people agreed and said that the key to Biggie's success was imitating Tupac from the ghetto narratives and the personal angst in his songs right down to the scarf tied around his head.

Professor William Jelani Cobb of Spelman College says, "I don't think that is a fair assessment. For one thing, Big was an extremely talented storyteller and Tupac never really crafted compelling narrative raps. Big probably had an edge in terms of his innovative deployment of vocabulary and word play, which was more of an east coast thing. West coast artists—with some notable exceptions—tended to de-emphasize double-entendre and pun in favor of visceral impact. Tupac had his own unique strengths in terms of conveying personal angst, but that trend didn't originate with either of them. Really, *Scarface* was talking about that kind of haunting subject matter before either of them."

Whatever the case, Tupac clearly was not ready to give up his grudge against Biggie. He would never forgive Biggie for failing to warn him in advance about the Quad ambush. For the rest of his life, he would insist that he had no friends.

When asked about his new boss, he told Sway, a radio interviewer with Oakland's KMEL radio, that he'd had at least one business dealing with Suge before his conviction. "I used to always see Suge. When they did the soundtrack for *Murder Was the Case* and I was going through all those legal problems. He was like, 'Yo give me a song, dog.' I gave him a song and I got the most I ever got for a song. It was damn near an album budget. I got something like $200,000 for one song and they didn't even use it. But I still got paid for everything I did for the sound track. I remember when he did it. He did it not because he was jacking me, but because he knew I was having crazy legal problems and I was a man. He had asked me to come to Death Row and I told him I wasn't ready. Instead of taking it personal he did that for me and I appreciated that."

Tupac was released from prison in October 1995. On November 30, 1995, twenty-seven-year-old Randy "Stretch" Walker met his end while driving his SUV on a neighborhood street close to his brother's home in Queens, New York. A black Acura had been following him, and someone opened fire with a high-powered rifle. Walker drove for his life. The SUV crashed and flipped over. Police investigators stated that before fleeing the scene, the assailants ensured the completion of the job by firing shots into the wreckage. It was one year to the day when he and Tupac had been assaulted at Quad Studios. Till the end, Walker had denied having anything to do with the incident at Quad Studios. Many immediately associated the date of Walker's murder with the Quad assault on Tupac and concluded that the murder was an act of revenge.

Tupac denied any knowledge of, or involvement in, the Walker shooting and started working to rebuild his shattered career.

thirty-seven

A PROBLEM BETWEEN
TWO RAPPERS

When Pac came to Death Row, other artists felt that Suge no longer cared about them. Suge said "that was childish on their part." It was not childish and the others had good reason to feel abandoned after Suge told a reporter, "You gotta understand . . . Tupac IS Death Row." Suge's first order of business was to get Afeni a house. He took Tupac to his first professional basketball game. There were trips to Mexico, Vegas, and Hawaii as well as gifts of cars and jewelry. Suge pampered Tupac and indulged his every whim . . . for a while.

In many ways, Suge Knight and Tupac Shakur were kindred spirits. For Knight's part, he was finally dealing with someone who'd challenge his own robust work ethic. The two men were laser-like in their intensity when it came to their work.

Knowing of the friendship between Tupac and Snoop Dogg, Suge gave Tupac a Rolls Royce as a celebratory gesture for Snoop Dogg's acquittal in his February 20, 1996, murder case. Life was good, but they were careful. Tupac sometimes wore a bulletproof vest and was constantly shadowed by at least one bodyguard. He made sure to never sit with his back to the door. Loud noises spooked him.

For a while Death Row was riding high but things changed drastically when Suge Knight lost sight of his vision. But for one very brief moment in the hip-hop sun, an entrepreneur named Suge Knight had sought to do something different. He invested his time and energy into hungry artists and then kept them well fed. He gave them comfort, a place to work, assured them that there was dignity in what they were doing, and promised that they were changing things for the better. He believed in, uplifted, and respected people who had gone through life being disrespected. He took their music and talent and made them wealthy celebrities, staying in the shadows and cheering them on as their stars rose.

By now everyone knew that Tupac and Biggie no longer had any contact with each other and that Tupac regarded him as a traitor. He had spent eleven months in jail, stewing over the whole mess and remembering how he helped Biggie build his fan base.

He angrily told a reporter, "I possess his soul. Let me tell ya something. They know that I was the truest nigga involved with Biggie's success. I was the biggest help. I was true. I didn't write his rhymes but he knows how I used to stop my shows and let him touch the show. I would let him blow up in the middle of my show. I used to buy him shit and give him shit and never ask for it back. I used to share. I'd share my experience in the (rap) game and the lessons and my rules and my knowledge of the game with him. Ya know what I mean? He owed me more than to turn his head and act like he didn't know some niggas were about to blow my fuckin' head off. He knew."

Should Biggie have warned Tupac not to come to Quad Studios that night? It would have been a huge risk on his part. He had warned Tupac over and over again that he was getting involved with a lot of shady characters and that he needed to distance himself from them. Tupac ignored his warnings and did what he wanted to do. If Biggie had told Tupac about the impending murder attempt, there is a good chance that Tupac would not have kept quiet about it. Once the gangsters found out that Biggie had "snitched," he would have been shot as well.

Biggie misunderstood Tupac on a very fundamental level. There were only a handful of people Tupac had ever called "friend." The most important were John Cole, Jada Pinkett, a guy called Mouse who lived in Baltimore, Shock G, and Biggie.

He genuinely cared about Biggie. Biggie apparently didn't understand that when Tupac said "friend," he meant a friendship that would last through thick and thin until their final breaths. He meant friend as in comrade, a common term that the Black Panthers had used to define their relationships with others in the struggle. Biggie wasn't that deep. When he said "friend," he probably meant "a great guy who I enjoy spending time with." With his perspective of friendship, it's likely that, had the situation been reversed, Tupac would have warned Biggie of the coming ambush irrespective of the risks to his own personal safety.

Biggie was in a no-win situation.

In the beginning, Tupac tried to explain that there was no East Coast/West Coast war. "It's just a problem between two rappers," he told reporters.

The media preferred its own version of the story and the public eagerly purchased the newspapers and magazines to read about the latest battle of the so-called war. Toward the end of his life, Tupac bought into the whole mess created by the media and said many incendiary things about people on the East Coast that were totally unnecessary and took the hostility to ever more toxic, dangerous levels. Biggie was no better. He bragged to a journalist that "one man against one man made a whole West coast hate a whole East coast, and vice versa."

Tupac admitted that "when I was in jail just sittin' there, I . . . was gonna quit rappin' but then Puffy and Biggie came out in *Vibe* magazine and lied and twisted the facts. All I wanted to do was end everything and walk away from the shit. I wanted to get out the game. I'm trying to get out the game and they wanna dirty up my memory. So instead of quittin' it made me wanna come back and be more relentless to destroy who used to be my comrades and homeboys."

There was more to the story. When the *New York Times Magazine* came out on January 14, 1996, the cover photo was of Suge Knight dressed in a red suit flanked by Tupac and Snoop. The article inside, written by Lynn Hirschberg, was hot. Suge told her that Tupac's outfit had been bought by the wife of a "top rapper." When asked who, Suge answered that it was Faith Evans, the wife of the Notorious B.I.G. But Suge didn't stop there, going on to explain that Faith had bought Tupac some other "stuff." When Hirschberg asked Tupac about the method of payment, he assured her with glinting eyes that Faith had been well compensated. He did everything but outright admit that he had slept with Biggie's wife.

Biggie was furious and made it clear that only one person was saving Tupac from his titanic wrath, and that person was Puffy Combs. "Puff don't get down like that," he said.

The 1996 Soul Train Awards were held in Los Angeles in March. Biggie picked up his award and thanked the people of Brooklyn for their support. The crowd booed him. Sadly, the fans were beginning to take sides in the ongoing feud.

Puffy was totally dismayed. "Tupac ain't mad at the niggas that shot him," he told an interviewer. "He knows where they're at. He knows who shot him. If you ask him, he knows, and everybody in the street knows, and he's not stepping to them, because he knows he can't get away with that shit. To me, that's some real sucker shit."

thirty-eight

CRUSADER

For many Americans, the term "hip-hop" evokes delight. Others, however, feel confused and repulsed. Hip-hoppers understand both reactions, but they are nevertheless determined to live life, rap their rhymes, and leave their impact in the way that is right to them and in a manner that secures their legacy.

There is nothing small about hip-hop. It possesses the power to electrify a crowd and the finesse to reach into the hearts of listeners. It can arouse them to great acts of creation, stir them to live out the largeness of their dreams, and remind them of the mournful but triumphant legacy that belongs to them as heirs and descendants of great struggles.

Hip-hop is a mega universe of attraction and contradiction where everything is large even when it is small. Few other art forms can boast of so many rags-to-riches stories. Few other examples can be found in the contemporary era of people who, understanding that life is short and time never stops, work so feverishly, consume so much, party so hard, and turn boldness into a fashion statement.

Self-anointed princes of the streets travel not with entourages but with posses. Battles in the boardroom and on the stage evolve into literal battles in the streets. Hard-sounding, beat-pounding, word-resounding masters of the mic are elevated to latter-day bards of the urban stage. There are no small egos. Grudges are announced and taken seriously. And no commentator of the craft is ever short of personalities to fill the roles of heroes and villains, kings and paupers, guns and snitches, those once hot and those who were not.

And so it was in the early 1990s, when gangsta rap had demonstrated that it could score huge sales for record companies. Among its critics were powerful luminaries like Harlem's Reverend Calvin Butts of the Abyssinian Baptist Church, who was the central figure in a protest at Sony Corporation's headquarters in midtown Manhattan. The event was caught on news cameras as Butts "dumped compact discs and cassettes of various gangsta rap artists onto the road" then "got behind the wheel of a bulldozer, crushed the albums, then delivered a speech accusing corporate hydras of profiting from music that celebrated black-on-black crime."

In 1993, Jesse Jackson, the leading mainstream political spokesperson for the black community, added his voice to the growing chorus of discontent, declaring that rap needed to be regulated and also lambasting the negative images perpetuated by the genre: "Anyone white or black who makes money calling our women 'bitches' and our people 'niggers' will have to face the wrath of our indignation."

But few people were as staunchly adamant and zealous in their disapproval as C. Delores Tucker as she led the charge to discredit the music. To accomplish her self-appointed task, she aligned herself with people who knew nothing about the dire conditions, grim reality, and ruthless socioeconomic disenfranchisement confronting black people in urban America.

It was said that along the way, Tucker attempted to score her own hustle. If this was true, it showed that she could be just as opportunistic and exploitative as the gangsta rappers she so vigorously opposed.

As the tenth of eleven children, born in Philadelphia on October 4, 1927, Cynthia Delores Nottage grew up with a strictly religious father, Bahamian-born Whitfield Nottage, and a "Christian feminist" mother, the former Captilda Gardiner. As the family entrepreneur, Captilda founded an employment agency for southern black migrant workers, ran a grocery store, and worked as a landlord. Tucker eventually inherited some of those properties. In 1966 she was identified as one of Philadelphia's most notorious slumlords, and her properties were eventually boarded up, taken over by the city, dispensed to charitable organizations, or abandoned.

She attended Temple University but left without a degree. In 1951, she married William Tucker, who owned a construction company and, over time, grew wealthy in real estate. She later sold real estate and insurance in Philadelphia, going on to immerse herself in the fight for civil rights. Whatever Tucker's later failings in life, her commitment to civil rights was sincere and inspired by ugly recollections of a direct encounter with bigotry and segregation when she was in high school.

Her father had gifted her with a trip to the Bahamas. She discovered that berths on the ship were segregated and refused to tolerate the inferior conditions assigned to minorities, choosing instead to sleep on the ship's deck. She was later diagnosed with tuberculosis and spent a year in bed. This effectively ruined her plans to attend college and pursue a medical career.

Like many blacks of that generation, Tucker had a confrontation with racism that inflamed her determination to resist, and in 1955 she joined the NAACP. Over the next decade, she marched with Martin Luther King Jr. in Selma and began working closely with Jesse Jackson. Her

involvement in civil rights led Tucker into Democratic politics. Over
the years she campaigned for black candidates and served on the Pennsylvania Democratic Committee, gaining a formidable reputation as a
fund-raiser and public speaker.

In 1971, Tucker was appointed secretary of the Commonwealth of
Pennsylvania by Governor Milton Shapp. She clearly enjoyed the prestige and power of her position and let the world know it by having the
number "3" emblazoned on the license plate of her state limousine to
show her ranking in state government.

Tucker's tenure in office was not without controversy, however, and
suggested that she was not averse to using her position for personal gain.
Some later revealed that her version of performing her duties primarily
involved raising her political profile more than working at her desk, but
she stayed in the job for six years. In 1977, allegations surfaced that she'd
been using state employees to write political speeches for which she'd
been paid. The price tag for "her" work was $66, 931. Governor Shapp
didn't need the negative exposure, so he fired her.

Ousted but not deterred, Tucker eventually sought political office,
running for lieutenant governor in 1978, the U.S. Senate in 1980, and the
House of Representatives in 1992. She never won office but remained
involved in politics and community affairs.

In 1984, Tucker, along with the venerable Shirley Chisholm, helped
to found the National Congress of Black Women. She also headed up
the minority caucus of the Democratic National Committee and was
a founding member of the National Women's Political Caucus. She
served for eleven years as chair of the Black Caucus of the Democratic National Committee and delivered addresses at five Democratic
conventions.

Judging from her résumé, C. Delores Tucker was certainly worthy
of being identified as a civil rights advocate, community activist, and
woman of great talent. However, her moments of ethical lapse made it

just as clear that she could be quick to exploit an issue or cause for her own gain.

For many, the gangsta rappers personified all of what was problematic in American society. Conversely, the members of the gangsta rap community, in so many words and ways, were indifferent that society recoiled at them and their lurid tales of mayhem, murder, and misogyny, which many found repugnant.

Many, citing the bold projections of gang life and gang culture, asserted that the gangsta rappers had invented gangsterism. But this was not the first time in America that artists had come under fire for bad taste and negative impact on society.

By the 1980s, Americans had spent decades nursing a fascination and revulsion, obsession and rejection of larger-than-life gangster crime figures. In the early decades of the twentieth century, during the silent film period (and long before the rise of gangsta rap), America had been feasting on the fare at Hollywood's table as moviegoers sat fascinated, watching tales of bad guy perpetrators.

In 1915, filmmaker D. W. Griffith released *Birth of a Nation*, which, in one of history's most egregious perversions of truth, depicted gangsters of the Ku Klux Klan as saviors of a post–Civil War South. The film tapped into popular hatred of blacks, showing beleaguered southern whites being victimized by black Federal soldiers (in the film, white men dressed up in blackface) as they cheated at the ballot box, fostered economic corruption, and stalked virginal young white women.

The astonishing success of Griffith's film inspired the rebirth of the Ku Klux Klan. By the mid-1920s, the Klan's resurgence was so pervasive and its power so expansive that it controlled state politics in Indiana; terrorized blacks throughout the South through lynching, fire-bombing, incessant harassment, and violence; and staged parades down Pennsylvania Avenue in Washington, D.C., in the backdrop of the United States Congress.

With the advent of sound films in the 1930s, America's appetite for gangster films became even more voracious. The sounds of gunfire, screeching tires, explosions, and screams added to the thrill of viewing audiences that made such films so popular.

From the start, Americans grumbled and groused about Prohibition and found a way of getting around the law. Americans who were determined to get their alcohol found ways of buying it; those who understood that drinkers wanted their booze, law or no law, broke the law to keep the boozers amply supplied. And since it was against the law, since Prohibition made alcohol a pricy and highly sought-after commodity, and since there was plenty of money to be made, the criminal underworld mobilized itself to ensure that the American thirst was slaked.

That led to certain conflict with law enforcement. Millions of alcohol-imbibing Americans, given the choice of rooting for the crooks who'd fulfill their desires or the cops who'd keep them sober and miserable in the bleak economic landscape of the Depression, chose the crooks. Hollywood, never failing to seize an opportunity to exploit a social reality, responded with gangster films that were instrumental in building the careers of stars like James Cagney, Edward G. Robinson, and Humphrey Bogart.

The first major gangster star, Edward G. Robinson, starred in *Little Caesar* (1930), the tale of a ruthless Chicago murderer loosely based on the life of Chicago mobster Al Capone, who rose rapidly to power, fortune, and fame, and fell just as quickly.

James Cagney's gripping performance as a cocksure, brutal, gun-slinging criminal bootlegger in *The Public Enemy* (1931) established him as a movie tough. His 1949 performance as psychopathic slayer Cody Jarrett, whose mother was the cold and murderously calculating leader of his gang, won him a permanent place of distinction in the genre of gangster films. For years to come, viewers sat mesmerized as Cagney, facing certain doom as law enforcement closed in on him, shouted "Top of the world, Ma!" while standing atop a massive gasoline storage tank that subsequently, and symbolically, exploded him into the flaming destruction he'd callously visited upon others.

Scarface: The Shame of a Nation (1932), produced by Howard Hughes, starred Paul Muni "as a power-mad, vicious, immature and beastly hood in Prohibition-Era Chicago." Muni's character, Tony Camonte, was, like the character in *Little Caesar*, loosely inspired by the murderous career of Al Capone.

Capone, who had proven to be a clear and present danger and ultimate menace to society, had nevertheless captured the imagination of filmmakers and moviegoers alike. Filmmakers profited from exploiting his crimes and moviegoers willingly paid to see their films. The landmark significance of the film stemmed from its inclusion of twenty-eight deaths, and the first use of a machine gun by a gangster.

In 1936, Humphrey Bogart made his screen debut in the *Petrified Forest*. His character, Duke Mantee, was inspired by notorious bank robber John Dillinger.

During the Depression many saw banks as the cause of their miseries, losing people's money and foreclosing on homes; this lent Dillinger and the rest of his gang the aura of modern-day Robin Hoods. Harry Pierpont, one of Dillinger's gang (which included outlaws like Baby Face Nelson, Bonnie and Clyde, and Machine Gun Kelly), once quipped, "I stole from the bankers who stole from the people."

But just as the gangsta rappers and Death Row Records would discover in the 1990s, not everyone during the 1930s was as willing to tolerate Hollywood's slavish glorification of violence, hedonism, debauchery, and anarchy. The Hays Production Code of the early 1930s curtailed glorification of criminals and the soft-gloved treatment given

to "ruthless methods and accompanying violence of the gangster lifestyle." After 1934, the censorship codes insisted that studios "make moral
pronouncements, present criminals as psychopaths, end the depiction
of the gangster as a folk or 'tragic hero,' de-glorify crime, and emphasize
that crime didn't pay."

Moral codes didn't end the production of gangster films, which continued to roll off of Hollywood's production line. In 1972, film history
was made with the release of Francis Ford Coppola's *The Godfather*.
This richly layered, masterfully told story lured audiences into the mul-
tigenerational tale of an Italian immigrant crime family that, aside from
merely showing bad guys running their "businesses" and "bumping off"
rivals, depicted the multiple realities of their existence.

In *The Godfather* and two sequels, audiences witnessed the rules of
loyalty, family and social hierarchy, the pleasures and price of power,
and the lethal consequences that always lurked for those who failed to
abide by the brutal code of the underworld.

In 1983, Al Pacino, who had prominent roles in all three *Godfather*
films, took on the role of Tony Montana in Brian de Palma's remake of
Scarface. Pacino's performance as a heartless, calculating Miami-based
Cuban immigrant drug lord boosted screen violence to bloodier levels.
The shock moviegoers might have experienced in 1932 by seeing twenty-
eight deaths in the first film was humane compared to the remake. Murder, lust, deception, butchery, and a plethora of guns, explosions, and
mayhem formed the landscape of the new film, which once more fed
America's taste for cinematic gangster carnage.

Although it has been said that the rappers at Death Row behaved as
if they were in a *Godfather* movie, the hip-hop nation has actually been
equally influenced by both *The Godfather* and *Scarface*. Toward the end
of his life Tupac was referring to Suge as the Don and himself "as just a
capo."

By 1989, alcohol had long been legalized and reinstated as America's drug of choice, and seemed innocuous compared to the new, more destructive drug called crack. In the 1991 movie *New Jack City*, Hollywood fed the public its artistic depiction of the raw realities of crack wars that were destroying urban families and neighborhoods.

Not to be left out, the music industry added its contribution to the social imaging and critiques in the form of gangsta rap. Some embraced the genre as a liberating testament to conditions that the rest of the nation refused to see. C. Delores Tucker and others excoriated it as the cause and perpetuation of the problems that, in truth and ironically, had produced it in the first place.

Tucker's initial disgust with gangsta rap stemmed from personal experience. A young female relative, Tucker's grandniece, wound up being ostracized when parents learned that the girl was using offensive language from a rap song. Upon investigation, Tucker deduced that the music was filled with lyrics and messages that glorified violence and degraded women.

Specifically, just as the howl grew louder about the violent gangland image portrayed by gangsta rappers connected with the Death Row label, the company did more to ensure that the images were burned deep into the public's imagination.

The negative publicity played right into Suge Knight's hands, elevating the street credibility and "realness" of Death Row Records and its artists. But there was a problem: most of the artists were not gangsters, recalled George Pryce, former Death Row director of communications.

Record producer Lionel Randolph pointed out that gangsta rap was like the movies and succeeded because drama sells. Even so, projecting a street-tough, battle-ready image didn't help gangsta rap sell itself as the answer to society's ills but rather declared an intent to worsen them. Club owner and DJ Alonzo Williams summed up the difficulty when he observed, "When you got brothers that's perpetrating . . . gang violence, or gang affiliation . . . that could be a problem."

It certainly was for C. Delores Tucker. Her first salvo against the gangsta rappers was a public relations campaign against the record stores that profited from selling gangsta rap. She demonstrated outside of retail outlets and was arrested in Washington, D.C., in 1993. She insisted that the music not be sold to minors and even urged the FBI to look into the matter. The Congressional Black Caucus held hearings on the effects of gangsta rap in 1994, the same year that Tupac Shakur was nominated for an NAACP Image Award for his role in the film *Poetic Justice* and in which Biggie Smalls released his popular debut album, *Ready to Die.*

Incensed, Tucker protested to the NAACP. As a board member, she was perfectly positioned to have her complaints heard. She also bought stock in Time Warner whose subsidiary, Death Row Records, produced some of the biggest names in gangsta rap. Tucker never saw *Poetic Justice* but nevertheless insisted that Tupac's being a gangsta rapper was more than enough reason to deny him the award, since he was teaching children to become criminals.

Unlike the self-righteous Tucker, California Congresswoman Maxine Waters, during the 1994 congressional hearings, challenged her colleagues to look into the message of the music and learn: "These are my children," she told them.

> I do not intend to . . . demean them. . . . I don't encourage the use of obscenities but don't lose sight of what the real problem is. . . . It is the reality they are rapping about. For decades, many of us have talked about the lives and the hopes of our people— the pain and hopelessness, the deprivation and destruction. Rap music is communicating that reality in a way that we never have.

Tucker wasn't moved. Being a shareholder in Time Warner, the owner of Interscope Records, which was parent to Death Row, allowed her to attend shareholders' meetings, where she expressed her ire with great passion. How long, she demanded to know, would Time Warner "continue to turn its back on the thousands of young people who were dying spiritually and physically due to the violence perpetuated in the [gangsta rap] recordings?"

Fully intent on reining in gangsta rap, Tucker established alliances with sixty black organizations. And just to prove that politics sometimes makes for truly unpredictable relationships, she joined forces with former George H.W. Bush administration drug czar William Bennett, leader of Empower America.

Tucker also welcomed assistance from Dan Quayle, whose greatest claim to fame had been to fulfill the role of vice presidential dud in the administration of George H.W. Bush. Senator Robert Dole, a World War II hero and presidential candidate in 1996, piled on, warning voters that society's fabric risked being shred to pieces by the gangsta rappers.

With such powerful help signing on to her war against gangsta rap, Tucker then changed strategy, deciding to fight the record labels rather than the artists. The dilemma for Time Warner was sticky indeed. By the time the pressure started really being felt, the company had invested millions into Death Row, and the return on the investment had been most handsome.

As Bruce Williams, a friend of Dre's, would later note, "They [Dre and Suge] helped to make street thug music the soundtrack of choice for America's youth. Tupac posters hanging on little white girls' bedroom walls was at least as shocking as Elvis gyrating on the *Ed Sullivan Show*."

So the crackdowns on gangsta rap began. Responses that cited freedom of speech were ignored or suppressed to focus on the allegedly destructive nature of the music. In fairness to the critics, gangsta rap's treatment of women was (and is) indefensible. Especially given the historical battles that black women have fought to maintain their dignity and respect, there is no excuse for verbally abusing them beneath the flimsy pretext of artistic culture.

Jesse Jackson struggled to understand how young black men could casually throw away the hard-won gains of the slaves who rebelled, the marchers who came later, the work of the great orators like Malcolm X and Fred Shuttlesworth, and the civil rights movement: "We always had the oppressor wanting to call our women bitches but we always fought against that. We didn't spread it. They called us niggers. We always fought against it. We didn't perpetuate it. Now we're getting paid to say that which we've always fought against."

Tupac Shakur's first album for Death Row, *All Eyez on Me*, released on February 13, 1996, highlighted Time Warner's dilemma as it squirmed before the critics while raking in staggering profits from the music. The album sold 566,000 copies in its first week, giving it the wherewithal to stand firm . . . for the moment.

From Tupac's point of view, the hypocrisy was infuriating: "Who do these fools think they're kidding?" he demanded to know on February 23, 1996, in a *Los Angeles Times* interview. "If these people actually cared about protecting the children like they say they do, they'd spend more time trying to improve the conditions in the ghettos where kids are coming up." Nevertheless, Time Warner had to carefully avoid the perception that it was caving in to Tucker and her growing army.

The mounting pressures from Tucker, Bennett, Dole, and Quayle moved Time Warner to urge Death Row chief Marion "Suge" Knight to delay the release of Snoop Dogg's *Dogg Food* album, which was expected to shoot to number one with multimillion-dollar sales. Pressure built until the negative publicity became too much for Time Warner and the company severed its relationship with Death Row, infuriating Suge Knight.

But Suge had never accepted defeat quietly. Death Row's parent company, Interscope, sued Tucker for attempting to interfere in contractual relationships. Next, Death Row sued Time Warner, Tucker, and Fuchs for "contractual interference, extortion, and violating the RICO [Racketeer Influenced and Corrupt Organizations] statute."

Tupac answered Tucker's rhetoric in the song "How Do U Want It": "Delores Tucker, you's a motherfucker/Instead of helping a nigga, you're trying to destroy a brother."

To elderly blacks who looked on him with disapproval, Tupac respectfully acknowledged their opinion but stuck to his guns: "No matter what y'all think about me, I'm still your child. You can't just turn me off like that."

In one final bizarre act, Tucker answered Tupac's complaints about her criticisms with one of her own in a lawsuit filed after Tupac's murder in which she charged that his lyrics had caused her such anguish that it had "diminished her sex life" to the point where she and her husband had not had sex for two years.

Lawyers for Tupac's estate replied with staid humor. "It's hard . . . to conceive how these lyrics could destroy her sex life. But we can only wait for the proof to be revealed in court." Noted journalist Nelson George called her charge "as gross and exploitive as anything Luther Campbell [a controversial rapper] ever recorded."

thirty-nine

PIGGIE AND BUFFY

upac and Snoop Dogg partied together and had some great times but they did more than just hang out. Theirs was a friendship with a special bond. When Snoop Dogg was on trial for murder, Tupac stood by him and tried not to miss court unless he had pressing business elsewhere.

Concerning Tupac's dedication, Snoop later said, "When I go back to that time, I remember someone whose friendship and love, courage and commitment, was like a gift from God to keep me going. When I walked through the valley of the shadow of death, there was someone by my side. His name was Tupac."

When Tupac joined Death Row, Snoop and Tupac were paired together on "2 of Amerikaz Most Wanted," a song featured on Tupac's fourth album, *All Eyez on Me*. The lyrics from that song showed a clear and profound shift in Tupac's lyrical content.

The opening message was clear: two of the best-known rappers in the United States, both vigorously pursued by the law, had wound up in the same place, rapping for the same record label, Death Row. Society, the law, and all of rap's detractors had not been able to keep them from merging their talent. By collaborating, Pac and Snoop were thumbing their noses at those who sought to silence them.

Of course, Snoop agreed with Tupac, admitting in his own smooth way that he was staying watchful of what the law would do, keeping his eyes open and being alert since he distrusted the authorities as much as they did him. But he admitted that "they got me on the run" and admitted to some angst as he described what life was like during the murder trial sitting "back in the courtroom waitin on the outcome."

In the next few lines, Snoop declared that he was about to fight back in a different kind of way. He was tired of being hassled by the law and social critics. To stay the hand of the former and silence the latter he would organize an event as impressive as the Million Man March.

Snoop suggested that he, his friend Tupac, and any other black man who had been labeled "gangster" needed a movement to fight against the powers that were allied with the people who were causing so much havoc for marginalized people.

Although Snoop and Tupac had become very rich, they were subjected to the same justice routinely meted out to the poor and powerless; they were just as vulnerable. But the question persisted: why and how was this possible if they were rich?

Their wealth had nothing to do with their difficulties with the justice system. The source of that difficulty (so they felt) had to do with their pigmentation rather than their bank accounts. Of course, it didn't help that Pac and Snoop sometimes invited trouble their way. But the main point was that no matter what, whether they'd caused the trouble or not, they were still black and therefore no better off than some poor joker from the hood. Tupac and Snoop next gave fair warning that as the pressures increased from the law and society, they were prepared to respond. Nothing was going to derail their plans. When Snoop said that he had "a house in the hills right next to Chino," he was noting that the house allowed him to overlook the California Institution for Men penal facility located in Chino, California. Just as the law was keeping an eye on him from all angles, he was also watching them.

At this point, Snoop admitted that while he'd gained access to the rich and famous by owning an automotive symbol of wealth, a Beamer (a.k.a. BMW), what he really wanted was to own a top of the line casino and be as powerful as the gangster Benjamin "Bugsy" Siegel.

Bugsy had begun life in the hard streets of Brooklyn and eventually found his way to the West Coast, where his criminal skills gained him entry into both the world of crime and Hollywood. Bugsy was a dapper dresser, had the prodigious skills of a seasoned lothario, and possessed a well-known mean streak. But despite his charm and his access to Hollywood high society, he was still a gangster. What mattered was that he was a gangster whom society seemed to tolerate and, in some circles, even revered.

So Snoop was poking society in the eye for its double-standard concerning him, Tupac, and other gangsta rappers. They were performers of a genre of music and were being castigated from one end of the country to the other. But real gangsters like Bugsy Siegel, who had been genuine threats to society, had done their business in the presence of and even with the collusion of the law. The implied question was, What's up with the unbalanced treatment? This was especially potent since the distinctions between a sociopath like Bugsy and performers like Pac and Snoop were so wide and apparent.

Tupac had used his fame to comment on the blistering conditions of his childhood and others of the dispossessed. When he rapped that "niggaz been dyin for years, so how could they blame us" he was challenging the law, and the nation, to explain the logic of putting upon him, Snoop, and gangsta rap in general, the onus of being responsible for crime. In effect, the violence that he'd been accused of creating had existed long before gangsta rap, and using him as a scapegoat had allowed society to distract itself from the real causes of violence—lack of education, poor housing, and overall poverty. Lambasting him as a villain did nothing to resolve pressing social ills.

After all of his run-ins with the law and being aware (as indicated in his previous lyrics) that he was being held responsible for crime in America, Tupac flatly pointed out that he lived in fear of a felony. In a truly transparent fashion, he admitted his fear of being locked up again and believed that the establishment would invent a charge in order to silence him. But even with all of that, he still intended to support friends who found themselves in trouble with the law.

Pac continued his commentary about feeling haunted by the law. The perspective of living on borrowed time was evident and he was telling all who would listen that people like him who come from backgrounds like his (i.e., the poor, the underprivileged, the destitute, and the desperate) and succeed anyway had better enjoy their success while they can.

Embedded in his verse was another realization: for some, making it big would never be good enough. They'd still be harassed. They'd still be stigmatized. They'd still be locked away. Pac was urging such persons to live large while they could before the law could ensnare them just as it had done, and was trying to do, to him and Snoop. Someone had declared them two of America's most wanted.

We can hear Tupac offering a truce. By asking for fifty feet, he wanted society and the law to get off of his back. But still, he wasn't going to be defeated. At the same time, his desire to be left alone by his detractors was powerful and he even offered to bargain with them, telling them that he just wanted to be free to return to the streets. He wanted to be back among his own, knowing that getting there was going to cost him something. That was undesirable but he was willing to let them keep whatever was left of him if they'd just finally, once and for all, back off.

At this juncture, Pac articulated the insanity that had so bedeviled his years and his world. People had let him down; friends who he thought should've been there for him weren't. Pac then told all who cared to know that anyone challenging him needed to understand that he was playing for keeps. Mercy was in short supply and, besides, it would take someone of special skills to "fade," or eliminate, a real thug like him.

A masterful summation of existence by Snoop got to the heart of life's issues. To live decently, it took money. Many youngsters growing up would have their first experience with sex before they'd had a chance to fully take in and understand the world. As a result, they ran the risk of increasing their hardship by creating permanent life situations in a world they still didn't understand. There were people working hard every day until they turned old and gray, and in the end they had little to show for playing by the rules. And since life's brutalities were just the way things were, Snoop mentioned that living by the gun was one way to even out the odds.

"2 of Amerikaz Most Wanted" was a terrific duet and a change of lyrical pace for both men. The song was a switch for Snoop because he hadn't been known as a political rapper and for Tupac since it was more gangsta than almost anything he'd done to date. Released on February 13, 1996, *All Eyez on Me* was Tupac's first album for Death Row Records; most importantly, it was hip-hop's first double album. It yielded lots of hits, including "California Love," "2 of Amerikaz Most Wanted," "How Do U Want It," and "Heaven Ain't Hard to Find."

The songs bear no resemblance to Tupac's earlier socially conscious work. It debuted at number one on the Billboard charts and sold more than a million units. David Browne's November 22, 1996, review for *Entertainment Weekly* said "Shakur has often made more compelling courtroom appearances (and movies) than records, but *All Eyez on Me* changes that dramatically. Shakur belongs on Death Row—the rap hit-factory label, that is, which is also home to Dr. Dre and Snoop Doggy Dogg. With a slew of producers, including Dre and nearly a dozen disciples of his g-funk sound, the album swings nonstop for over two rambunctious hours. Crammed with Egyptian-snake-charmer key-boards, creamy choruses chanted by wet-lipped women, and police whistles used musically, the arrangements burst with sonic detail; two speakers don't seem capable of containing it all."

But it was the video for "2 of Amerikaz Most Wanted" that caused the controversy. It had nothing to do with the lyrics of the song. It was Tupac's revenge fantasy against Puffy and Biggie. At the start, a bloody Tupac, flanked by two henchmen, walks in on a conversation between two people called "Buffy" and "Piggie." The two are celebrating what they believe to be the successful assassination of Tupac. When Pac walks in with his left arm in a sling, blood splattered over his shirt, and looking shaken but strong, Piggie and Buffy are clearly rattled.

"Pac!" Piggie blurts out in shocked surprise. "You alive? I mean, you safe?"

After a few moments of stammering and stuttering, Piggie and Buffy express relief that Tupac is all right. Then the phone rings several times. Pac's searing eyes glance down at the phone and he asks Piggie if he's going to answer. Piggie finally gets the phone and has a brief, nervous conversation with someone whose voice is male and says, "We did it, man!"

Tupac asks Piggie who was on the phone and Piggie says that it was his wife, Faith, who was supposedly always calling to check up on him. Pac knows the truth and reaches inside his sling for a pack of cigarettes. Piggie, thinking that Pac's making a move for a pistol, cries out, "Pac, please don't kill me. It was Buff's idea. I'm just a rapper. Please don't take me out the game." Buffy likewise pleads for his life.

Pac lights up his cigarette and says to Piggie, "I ain't gonna kill you. We was homeboys once, Pig. Once we homeboys, we always homeboys."

Piggie and Buffy both express relief that Pac's going to let them live. Neither explains their leaping to the conclusion that Pac was about to shoot them for their part in his near assassination. This self-confession to an offense that Pac never mentions removes all doubt that "Piggie" and "Buffy" were connected to the attempt to murder him.

This music video now serves as part of a video archive that, at least for this incident in his life, explains to the world the truth—as he saw it—regarding the attempt on his life on November 30, 1994. In stark terms that cannot be misinterpreted, Pac communicated that he had no illusions about what really happened that night.

At the end of the scene, Tupac steps back as two henchmen, flanking either side of him, step forward to kill Buffy and Piggie.

forty

THE SECOND SHOOTING

Frank Alexander, author of *Got Your Back: Protecting Tupac in the World of Gangsta Rap*, started working for Death Row in September 1995, the month Tupac Shakur was released from prison. While working as lobby security at Can Am Studios where Death Row acts recorded, Alexander found Glocks, 9-millimeters, Bowie knives, and other weapons. On such occasions (and they were frequent) he simply asked the owners of the weapons to return the items to their car. There was grumbling but everyone complied. Rules about marijuana were different. "Bags and bags of pot flowed into Can Am, like there was an endless train unloading at the doorstep."

Suge liked to use his massive size in dealing with people, letting it speak in ways that made words unnecessary. But with Frank, he had another person who had cultivated himself into a wall of power. Everyone who met Frank was taken aback by his massive build and size. From a business perspective, especially with the tough street rep that Death

Row cultivated, having Frank on board made perfect sense. He looked like a bench-pressing warrior who could take any man down.

Over time Frank got to know the other security people, most of whom had backgrounds in law enforcement like him. Kevin Hackie was a Compton police officer who'd worked with Reggie Wright (owner of Wrightway Security, and Frank's boss), and they had a ten-year history together on the police force. Reggie Wright's father, Reggie Wright Sr., had a high-ranking position as lieutenant in Compton, and Kevin knew him as well.

What Frank didn't know when he accepted the job was that real criminals had started hanging around the Death Row offices and were doing what real criminals did. The company was on its way down.

Frank and a few members of the Death Row contingent flew into New York on a Friday and stayed in a New Jersey Ramada Inn, across the Hudson River. Death Row people weren't used to staying in such common surroundings, but Suge Knight had his reasons. He wanted to ensure that the artists didn't get into mischief, and the location was thirty miles from Manhattan. To get downtown was expensive and time-consuming, limousines were in short supply, and the snowy weather added another deterrent. Suge was serious about there being no trouble.

Alexander met with Snoop the following morning. As he and five others strolled into Snoop's room, they were met with the distinctive odor of marijuana. Inside the room, Snoop's dad, Vernon, and his Uncle Reo were both laid back and having fun, so everyone seemed to be getting along.

They spent the day in Times Square, getting material for the video. That night Snoop was scheduled to be the special guest at a popular local radio station.

Before they arrived, Biggie called the station and asked to be put on the air. Once that was done, he said, "I cannot believe that New York is allowing Snoop, Tupac, and Tha Dogg Pound to shoot a video in Times Square. What kind of shit is this?"

"This is our city," he railed, adding that "you know the beef we have with these muthafuckas."

The call from Biggie caused an immediate chill at the radio station. The DJ, clearly rattled, couldn't decide whether or not to let Snoop into the studio. When he finally agreed, Snoop had changed his mind and started heading back to the Ramada.

After all of the prior coordination with the station manager, one phone call from Biggie had put a hold on everything. Snoop was disgusted and returned to his room, where he played video games. But that was Snoop: cool and laid back.

Later, it was back to the trailer in Times Square to shoot the video. The gunshots came from across the street, "right in front of a corner storefront." The target was the trailer. Alexander's reflexes took over, and, without a vest on, he lunged into Snoop's trailer with gun in hand and started yelling, "Where's Snoop?"

The people in the trailer were frozen in fear and he started pulling them out, one at a time. Security mobilized quickly and Alexander frantically checked to see who was there and who might be missing. Everyone was shaken but okay. At last he found Snoop. When the shooting had started, everyone "dogg-piled on top of him."

"You okay, you okay?" Alexander asked Snoop.

The unflappable rapper answered with a simple, "Yeah, I'm all right."

Frank then turned his attention to getting his charges away from danger. He muscled them all, one by one, into the security van. After a frenzied ride, with the van driving toward the danger at one point rather than away from it, they got away safely.

Alexander has said that Biggie was mistaken. "Tupac was not with us. It was Snoop and the Dogg Pound." He also added that whoever shot into that trailer was not firing warning shots. "They were shooting in there to kill somebody."

When Tupac heard the story, he immediately decided that he wanted Frank to be his bodyguard exclusively. Suge agreed and Frank ended up working for Tupac.

Tupac's nickname for Alexander was "Big Frank," and he seemed to take great relief in having him by his side.

Until then, Biggie had steered clear of the media and let his harsh feelings float back to Tupac through the music industry grapevine. This had the desired effect of making the loud, fast-talking, media-friendly Tupac appear to be the only one playing this dangerous game, while Biggie bravely endured his insults with dignity. It was a brilliant strategy that made Tupac look paranoid and hyperaggressive by comparison. The fact that Biggie made such an incendiary phone call to the media suggests that he was enraged to the point of becoming unglued.

forty-one

BLACK ROYALTY AND BIG PLANS

Quincy Jones was born on Chicago's South Side on March 14, 1933. His mother, Sarah Frances, struggled with schizophrenia and had to be institutionalized for part of his childhood. His father, Quincy Delight Jones Sr., worked as a carpenter but also played semiprofessional baseball.

Quincy was ten when his family moved to Bremerton, Washington, a suburb of Seattle. He started playing the trumpet after trying all of the instruments in the school band. During his teenage years he formed a musical partnership with another talented musician named Ray Charles, who was three years older. Together they performed at small club events and weddings.

In 1951, when Quincy was eighteen, he was awarded a scholarship to the prestigious Schillinger House in Boston, Massachusetts, which was known for training classical musicians. Obtaining the scholarship was a clear sign of Quincy's great talent, but his musical heart was drawn in other directions and he dropped out when he was offered the opportunity to go on the road with jazzman Lionel Hampton.

Displaying the sharp instincts that would serve him well in his future musical and business endeavors, Quincy took the offer. The lessons he learned came in handy when he moved to New York and started working as a freelance musical arranger for talents like Sarah Vaughan, Count Basie, Duke Ellington, and his old friend, Ray Charles.

By 1956 Quincy was trumpeter and music director for a band led by Dizzy Gillespie. This was the period of the cold war, and America had just three years earlier agreed to a rickety cease-fire in Korea. Suspicions of spies at home had cast a pall over American society and heightened tensions in the Atlantic community of nations. In this troubled atmosphere Dizzy Gillespie, along with Quincy and the band, traveled throughout the Middle East and South America as ambassadors of American goodwill, talent, and artistic freedom.

The tour was a success, and Quincy then began recording big band albums for ABC Paramount Records with himself as the bandleader. Ever in search of good musical talent, trends, and associations, he moved to Paris in 1957 and studied composition with Nadia Boulanger and Olivier Messiaen. Since his energy seemed boundless, he also worked as a music director for Mercury Records' French distributor, Barclay Disques, and then went on another road tour as musical director of Harold Arlen's jazz musical *Free and Easy*.

When the European tour closed in February 1960, Quincy got together with some band members from the Arlen show and formed his own eighteen-member big band. They went on the road with their families in tow and earned rousing applause and rave reviews at home and in Europe. Their operating costs outdistanced profits, however, and the band dissolved, leaving Quincy with a great deal of debt.

With some help from Irving Green, the head of Mercury Records, Quincy took care of his financial problems and returned to New York as music director for the label. It worked out well for him. In 1964, he was named VP of Mercury Records, becoming the first African American to hold an executive position in a white-owned record company. At this juncture Quincy turned his attention to another area long closed to blacks: film scoring. He would go on to compose music for over thirty films.

By the 1960s, television had established itself as a titanic media entity and Quincy became part of that powerhouse community as well. He scored the themes for *Ironside, Sanford and Son,* and *The Bill Cosby Show.*

Quincy also immersed himself in the struggle for civil rights. He was an avid supporter of Dr. Martin Luther King's Operation Breadbasket, which sought to promote economic development in America's inner cities. After King's assassination, Quincy served on the board of Jesse Jackson's Operation PUSH (People United to Save Humanity).

Quincy's work as a musician and collaborator on film and television projects established him as a towering figure in entertainment. But his life almost ended in August 1974, when he suffered a cerebral aneurysm. After undergoing two delicate operations and spending six months recuperating, Quincy Jones was back doing what he loved and working harder than ever.

In 1982, he collaborated with Michael Jackson on the album *Thriller,* which became the best-selling album of all time and also broke MTV's color barrier.

Tupac criticized Quincy in print because of his preference for white women. Quincy's response was benign: "I said okay here is a loose cannon. I've known hundreds of those or thousands of those." One of his daughters was not nearly as generous. Rashida Jones wrote a stern letter to *Vibe* magazine and followed up with one to Tupac that said in part, "How could you even criticize his personal life when if it weren't for people like him you wouldn't even be here. And where are you gonna be in ten years? Dead or in jail?"

Tupac was at a celebrity party when he thought he spotted Rashida in the crowd. The woman turned out to be Rashida's sister, Kidada. He tried again and again to get her attention so that he could apologize for being so boorish. For her part, Kidada could not understand why Tupac would not stop following her—until she remembered the article.

After she explained that he had mistaken her for her sister, they shared a laugh and spent some time together. It wasn't long before they were dating. Sometime later when Quincy took Rashida to meet Kidada at a restaurant, he noticed Tupac sitting in a booth. He grabbed the young man's shoulders from behind and shouted "TUPAC!"

Tupac was rattled, all the more so when Quincy told him that he wanted to have a private word with him. The two of them went into a corner and worked out their differences. Tupac apologized for hurting the family and expressed his genuine love for Kidada.

Quincy became a friend. To Tupac's delight, Kidada's mother, 1970s TV actress Peggy Lipton, liked him too. She says, "Tupac was charming, especially toward older women.

By late April 1995, Tupac and Kidada were living together in his Calabasas, California, mansion. Kidada Jones (who had previously dated LL Cool J) was black royalty and she was gorgeous. Tupac had come a long way, but many people in his entourage didn't like her.

Perhaps it was as simple as her being a product of her environment. She had been born on March 22, 1974, approximately three years after Tupac. Like him, she had a troubled youth but for different reasons. Tupac was emotionally troubled because he had had to deal with issues like lack of food, clothing, shelter, and personal safety. There was also the parental drug addiction and the expectation that he live up to his South American name and save the black community.

Kidada was a rich girl who chose to live with her father in his Bel Air mansion when her parents divorced. But she had her own unspecified issues, and they had caused her to be kicked out of eleven schools by the age of fifteen.

Rapper LL Cool J ended his relationship with Kidada upon discovering that she consulted gurus, prayed to statues, and engaged in strange rituals that involved spiritual leaders conducting prayers by stroking believers with feathers. After one such encounter, LL got out . . . fast!

"It was not about disrespecting Kidada," he later observed. "It was more about me respecting and connecting with God on a level where I felt comfortable. We [he and Kidada] weren't on the same wavelength. . . . I was from Queens, she was from Bel Air. I know what it's like to be hungry and live on the subway, all she's ever known is being rich. She has a rich, successful, talented father. My father was mostly absent. She praised a guru and statues, and I praise God, straight up. . . . So, we went our separate ways."

Divergent backgrounds notwithstanding, Tupac and Kidada connected and nothing else mattered. After his stint in jail Tupac went frantically in search of acting work. Vondie Curtis-Hall, who directed *Gridlock'd*, recalled that Tupac "hounded me down."

The rapper wasn't Curtis-Hall's first choice but Tupac was determined. Once they met, Tupac showed Curtis-Hall the same passion and intensity that he'd used to get his role in *Juice* and the deal was made.

Tim Roth, Tupac's costar, was mortified to learn Tupac had gotten the part. He even went so far as to warn Curtis-Hall, "Don't do a movie with that . . . guy. You'll get shot on the set."

After a meeting with Tupac, Roth was on board.

In one of the early scenes of *Gridlock'd*, Tupac had difficulty getting his part right, which frustrated him to no end. Tupac and Roth, playing two addicts trying to kick their drug habits, sit on the side of the bed where Thandie Newton lies dying from an overdose.

Tupac's character has an epiphany at that moment and decides to change his life. He has to ask the question, "Do you ever feel like your time is running out?"

Indeed, Tupac seemed to be racing through life with the urgency of a man whose time would run out sooner than anyone anticipated. His eyes often seemed filled with a depthless pain that had its origins in disasters and traumas from years before. It was a part of him, and it burdened him all the days of his short life. Everyone who knew him remembers his extraordinary work ethic and wondered, What makes Tupac run?

In the beginning he ran to get away from his Dickensian childhood of impoverishment and humiliation. After dropping the T.H.U.G. L.I.F.E. campaign, he ran from the demand that he pick up the Black Panther Party's fallen banner and lead his people to freedom and victory over social injustice. Now he was about to run away from gangsta rap.

Tupac had big plans: start a label, do more films, marry Kidada, and move out of Los Angeles so that the kids could be raised away from the glare of celebrity.

In an interview on Oakland's KMEL radio, he acknowledged that every time he got up, something or someone had always knocked him back down, "It's like the twilight zone. It's like some evil, unstoppable shit that won't let me go. It's got its hands on me and it wants to see me fail. In my mind sometimes when I'm drunk or I'm just laying down. . . . I keep thinking to myself, Damn is this true? . . . Am I gonna fail? Am I supposed to fail? Should I just stop trying and give up? . . . But it's a game. It's the game of life. . . . I know one day they're gonna shut the game down but I gotta have as much fun and go around the board as many times as I can before it's my turn to leave."

When the interviewer asked where he saw himself in five years, he mentioned helping Suge Knight and Death Row as the A&R person. But all of that had to wait until after his next record. It was his last kick to Biggie's stomach, and it was called *Hit Em Up*.

forty-two

THE NOTORIOUS P.I.S.S.E.D.

Tupac put it on wax. The first line of "Hit Em Up" is "That's why I fucked your bitch you fat muthafucka," and it got worse from there. By the end of the song, Tupac had threatened Biggie, Puffy, Lil Kim, and everyone else associated with Bad Boy Records.

Professor Michael Eric Dyson has written that "Tupac released the most bitter, vindictive, vengeful battle rap and diss song of all time which was called 'Hit Em Up' where he begins to literally talk about having sex with Biggie's wife so it was ingenious and it was evil. It was vicious and it was powerful and compelling at the same time."

Dyson's was a generous assessment. "Hit Em Up" was not a battle record. It was not a song. It shouldn't even be called music. It was simply rage unhinged.

The May 1996 issue of *Vibe* magazine included an article written by Karen R. Good, entitled "Faith. Fully." When asked if she had sex with her husband's enemy, Faith denied it. Faith told Good that she was in Los Angeles right after Tupac was released from prison. While she was out with friends, Treach of Naughty by Nature spotted her and told her

223

that Tupac wanted to have some words with her. It was supposed to be just a friendly "Hi," nothing more. So they talked.

Tupac expressed his admiration for her work, suggested that they work together sometime, and Faith agreed. "He was mad cool. I saw him at a couple of parties, and we was chillin' havin' drinks, him and my friends."

To passersby who knew of the poisoned blood between Tupac and Biggie, Faith must've seemed oblivious, uncaring, or cynically tempting fate.

She went on to say that he asked her to record a song with him and she did. She then stated that she hadn't seen or heard from him since her Los Angeles trip "and if I saw him, I don't know what I would do or say."

In her autobiography *Keep the Faith* (2008), she paints a far different picture of the hours that she spent in Tupac's presence. Despite the fact that Tupac's signing with Death Row was covered by every major news outlet in the country, she claims that she didn't know about it until they reached the recording studio and she saw a Death Row Records sign over the door. The Tupac in her book is definitely not "mad cool." In fact, they are alone in his hotel room (a detail that she may or may not have told Karen Good) when he refuses to pay her and gets quite nasty. "You know you want to suck my dick, bitch. Don't fucking lie," he says. Plus, despite the fact that the Biggie/Tupac feud was one of the biggest stories in the music industry, she claims not to have known that the two men were mad at each other. "But ... but ... I ... thought y'all was friends," I said.

Faith wrote that Biggie went ballistic after hearing "Hit Em Up." He showed up at her hotel room and started banging on the door. She let him in and he repeatedly shouted, "Did you fuck him?" over and over again even as she repeatedly denied it. He tossed things around and continued to rant and rave until she just wished he would do whatever he came to do and get it over with, even if it meant her life. Finally, she fled into the bathroom and didn't come out until he was gone.

Biggie would have been even angrier if he had known that Tupac was also screwing his mistress, an up-and-coming rapper whom Biggie had renamed Charli Baltimore.

"Hit Em Up" did not scare Puffy, who pointed out that the talkers usually don't do anything: "Bad boys move in silence. If somebody wants to get your ass, you're gonna wake up in heaven. There ain't gonna be no record made about it. It ain't gonna be no interviews; it's gonna be straight up, 'Oh Shit, where am I? What are these wings on my back?'"

Even in the midst of his rage, Biggie could not understand Tupac's ensuring that Faith was personally wounded if the intent had been to get at him. "If honey was to give you the pussy," Biggie told an interviewer, "why would you disrespect her like that?" He went on to say that he believed his wife but there was little else that a man in his position could say and still maintain face. Biggie was still angry when he recorded a tune that said if Faith (who was pregnant) had twins, it would probably be Two Pacs.

The security people at Death Row had a lot of security meetings, but no one warned the bodyguards about "Hit Em Up," the song that basically declared war on the East Coast. Frank learned about it when he heard it on his car radio. His wife was in the car too. They'd just had a nice dinner and were heading home. Frank could not believe what he was hearing. The number of words that had to be bleeped from the song was ridiculous. There seemed to be more bleeps than words in the vitriolic rap.

By the time Alexander got into his house, the phone was already ringing.

He answered and heard the voice of Reggie Wright, asking if he'd heard the song. Frank quickly got to the point: "Reggie, we are going to need two bulletproof vests; we're gonna need to have more than me as a bodyguard for Pac, and you know that. I'm going to talk to Pac, and we need to talk to Suge."

The next day, Alexander asked Tupac what on earth had gotten into him. Tupac feigned ignorance by answering with an innocent, "What?"

"On the real, Pac," Alexander urgently explained. "You need to talk to Suge. We got to up your security. This song is gonna create a lot of trouble and there's gonna be a lot of places we're going, when we're gonna need more than just one set of eyes."

Tupac laughed off Alexander's concern, playing him a recording of "Hit Em Up" instead and bragging about how the rap was going to be known everywhere. He seemed totally disinterested in the chaos the song would cause and about what it meant for his safety, though that didn't deter Alexander from trying to get him more security.

At a later meeting with fifteen other security persons at Suge's house in Malibu, Alexander insisted, "We need more guards working with Pac."

"Yeah, you're right," Suge agreed. "But he don't like anybody but you."

That was good to hear. Tupac was Death Row's prize, and it was good to know that he was favored by the company's most valuable star. But that star also had painted a huge bull's-eye on himself with "Hit Em Up" and that was troubling in the extreme.

Tupac was Alexander's responsibility and it was going to remain that way. All of the other security guys had listened to "Hit Em Up" and each one decided that he wanted to be kept as far away from Tupac as possible.

The day he got to Can Am recording studio from prison, he "banged out" *All Eyez on Me,* which became his first album for Death Row and eventually went double platinum. Alexander's longtime friend K. J. told him that Tupac did the first six tracks in one night. And all the while, the rapper was shooting videos and flying to award shows.

The pace Tupac kept was nothing short of amazing. If he found that he'd lived into the next day, he kept hustling as though the new day was his new last one. When he finished *All Eyez on Me,* he went on tour across the country with Tha Dogg Pound but was already work-ing on *The Don Killuminati: The Seven Day Theory*, using his Makaveli pseudonym.

That album was released two months after his death. In November 1996, David Browne of *Entertainment Weekly* reviewed the album:

The Don Killuminati/The 7 Day Theory, credited not to 2Pac but to an alter ego, Makaveli. In this regard, Death Row has done right by him: If Shakur were alive to hear this mess, he wouldn't want his name on it, either. . . . Posthumous records are old news in the music business, but *The Don Killuminati* truly feels like a work in progress . . . if Shakur had been planning an album playing off Machiavelli's theories on power, he neither thought it through nor completed it. The songs have only fleeting refer-ences to "Makaveli" and occasional bits of Machiavellian advice ("Keep your enemies close/Nigga, watch your homies"). . . . Dr. Dre and his posse livened up Shakur's previous album, *All Eyez on Me*, but with Dre gone from Death Row, lesser-known producers were called in. The results are plodding, amateurish gangsta rap. The album is top-heavy with cameos from second-rate rappers, and the depths of absurdity are reached on "Toss It Up," which grafts a vitriolic Shakur rap onto a standard new-jack strut. *The Don Killuminati* isn't just a mop-up operation; it's a disgraceful exploitation that dishonors Shakur's music and legacy . . . it's important to remember that Shakur had a cultural legacy. In the world of hip-hop, success comes with a price: Ac-quire too much fame and wealth and your friends start wonder-ing if you've lost touch with the streets. The only remedy is to act harder. . . . Put-downs have always played an important role in rap. But on this shameful cash-in, Tupac Shakur is the only one truly being dissed.

Tupac also began working on *Gridlock'd* while shooting one video a week with the movie in full production. Needless to say, it took some effort keeping up with him and his twenty-four-hour days! People would sometimes ask how it was all being done and Alexander would blandly reply, "We're just doing it."

But there was something pushing Tupac; it was something that he had to do and Alexander suspected that no matter what he told the media, it had much to do with the rapper's desire to pay his debt to Death Row and be free.

Frank watched Tupac have as much fun as a man could want:

"Tupac enjoyed himself," Frank later said. "He did everything that he wanted to do. The good life was his for the moment, and he had fun. He played . . . he made money, he traveled, he smoked weed," and, of course, he enjoyed the company of many, many women. "He did everything that someone would do if it was the last year of their life, and he was good at all of it."

In his typical last-minute kind of way, Tupac informed Frank that they had to go to Italy and that Frank needed to bring another bodyguard with them. Kidada would be going too. After one recruiting attempt fizzled in a dispute about money, Frank convinced another Death Row bodyguard named Michael Moore to take the trip.

Tupac was satisfied with Alexander's selection and off they went. What was also telling was Tupac's insistence that he get more round-the-clock security. If he didn't suspect lurking danger, he certainly acted like he did.

The trip to Italy was arranged through the offices of Quincy Jones. He was handling it for *Vibe* magazine, which he partly owned. Carla, Kidada's friend in *Vibe* public relations, took care of all the details. Once Alexander learned what they'd be doing and when, he was flabbergasted: "In just a couple of days, Pac was going to be in twelve fashion shows, as well as after parties. It [the schedule] was insane."

For Tupac, who loved being around women, Italy was paradise. All of the women were beautiful, and not just the supermodels. Tupac especially loved their eyes and Alexander understood why: "Eyes on women in Italy were unlike any you find in America. They came in colors I'd never seen before, and combined with their skin tone, so many of them were drop-dead gorgeous."

Being in Italy got Tupac's party juices flowing. But not everyone was feeling it, especially Kidada who wanted to keep her rapper boyfriend on schedule and focused on his business. Finally, during a ride back to the hotel, Tupac protested: "I'm . . . tired of doing everything y'all want me to do. I've done everything on the schedule to the letter, and when do I get to have my fun?"

Thus unburdened, he was like the proverbial chocoholic in the chocolate factory. He had come from nothing, climbed to the top of the music world, and found himself in Italy amid some of the most beautiful women on the planet. Tupac went nuts, enjoying himself in ways that had been denied him for a long time.

forty-three

THE THIRD SHOOTING

ow that he had gotten revenge against Biggie with "Hit Em Up," Tupac was ready to run from another, far more dangerous role, which he'd grown tired of playing. Gangster.

It was going to be a good time. Tupac Shakur was coming to Las Vegas to see his friend Iron Mike Tyson, the terrorizing pugilist from Brooklyn, fight Bruce Seldon. Many didn't expect the contest to last long. Afterward, there'd be much partying.

The day prior to Tupac's arrival, September 6, 1996, Frank checked into Death Row's Vegas hotel of choice, the Luxor. Preparations had to be made before the rapper got there and Frank was on the case.

It was a fight weekend. The normally large crowds in Vegas were sure to be that much bigger. Tupac was coming to town. He'd have his entourage. Suge Knight and the Death Row posse were going to be stomping through as well. Stars of all types would be on hand being beckoned by armies of groupies and fans who'd be pressing, pushing, and pleading for a moment of celebrity time.

A security meeting was called for noon. Every security person in attendance understood that the next twenty-four to forty-eight hours were going to tax them to the edge of their skills.

Despite all of their attempts to prepare, no one was ready for the directive that no weapons would be allowed in Suge Knight's 662 Club after the fight. They could leave them in their rooms (which was pointless), or they could leave them in their vehicles if they insisted on having their weapons close by. But the word was final: no guns in the club.

Security people guarding stars needed all of the tools of their profession. It wasn't like danger didn't hover close by. Sam Cooke, John Lennon, and even presidents had been murdered by dangerous people nobody saw coming. Others had had their lives threatened. It was an occupational hazard: sometimes the people who claimed to love the stars most were the ones who did them the most harm.

The only other times when security had been told to go unarmed was, understandably, aboard airplanes. There was grumbling and consternation, but orders were orders so weapons would be left in the vehicles.

Frank continued making sure that all was ready for Tupac's arrival. The idea of going without his weapon at the club after the fight didn't sit well. But doing that would be a challenge since Kevin Hackie (who has since confessed that he was an undercover FBI agent during the entire time that he worked on security guard assignments at Death Row), who'd been guarding Tupac during Frank's recent vacation, had failed to leave Frank's radio available to pick up for when he'd be in Las Vegas.

It was challenging enough guarding Tupac on a good day when everything went right and all tools were available. The weekend was guaranteed to be a zoo with much going wrong and the bodyguard's two most important assets, his weapon and communications, weren't going to be available. There was no time to complain. Tupac would be arriving on the seventh and Frank had to make the best of it.

Tupac, elusive, impulsive, and free-spirited, arrived in town and had to be hunted down by his bodyguard. Since Death Row's crew preferred the Luxor Hotel it was a short hunt and Frank found Tupac in the casino gambling.

"Big Frank!" Tupac yelled to his friend and protector.

Tupac kept gambling, winning money. People pressed in from all around. Everyone wanted to get a look, a glance, or a glimpse of Tupac, whose life had taken on mythic proportions. Frank, Michael, and Tupac's backup group, the Outlawz, worked to keep the crowd back. As was his way, Tupac suddenly decided that he wanted something different. That something different was over at the MGM, but he was also wondering where Suge was.

Frank urged him to wait until he could call Reggie Wright and find out Suge's location. It was a short call. Reggie had to get back with Frank about Suge's whereabouts and when he'd most likely be at the Luxor. Frank hurried back to share the news with Tupac but he was gone. In the time that they'd known each other Tupac had rarely left the range of Frank's watchful eyes.

A frantic search through the hotel yielded nothing. Tupac Shakur, a star of stars, was on his own without security. Frank found him at the Luxor. He was still restless and still upset that Suge hadn't arrived.

He wanted to do something, but what? Tupac seemed driven to be on the move, to be active, to not wait, to keep in motion so that he'd stay in motion. He schemed with Frank and fellow security Michael Moore that they should all get dressed before going back to the MGM.

It was Tupac's show. The bodyguards were there to follow him; if the MGM was where he wanted to be then they'd be there also. So they changed clothes, met back up, and caught a cab over to the MGM.

Tupac caught a cab to a place well within walking distance when he otherwise would have walked. At the MGM, bodyguard senses went overload. The place was a madhouse of people. The madness was caused by the mere appearance of Tupac, loving the attention and having the time of his life.

But hours were passing and the Tyson fight was approaching. Everyone had to get to their seats, and Suge still hadn't arrived. Tupac was pissed. Suge's penchant for fashionably late imperial entries could be grating and this member of his royal court had grown tired of the drama.

MGM security guided the rapper and his associates back to the grand arena area. On the way, there were more people to be shooed away to give the rapper room. Seven-thirty came and went but there was still no Suge, so Tupac paced and fumed. "I didn't want to come here anyway," he griped. And he really hadn't. Tupac's original plan had been to go to Atlanta and settle some issues with relatives, but Suge had gotten his friend to change his plans.

But there were other reasons too: "Tupac's reason for being at the Tyson-Seldon fight went beyond friendship. Tyson's walk to the ring was always accompanied by rap music. For a long time, Public Enemy was the heavyweight champion's music of choice. But on this night, it was Tupac. The rapper had written a song, 'Wrote the Glory,' that Tyson played during his entrance. (Tyson had also entered the ring for other fights to the Tupac song 'Ambitionz az a Ridah.')"

Along with the satisfaction of hearing his music pumping up a fight crowd and that generation's most feared boxer, a definite highlight of the trip was Kidada Jones, and Tupac planned on taking her to Suge's 662 Club after the fight. That way, she wouldn't be in the midst of the rowdies at the fight and they could have a good time together later on.

Tupac was reaching his limit. He demanded to know where Suge was. So Big Frank called Reggie again, explaining with measured urgency that the rapper was getting steadily wound up. As he talked, Tupac came and stood with him at the pay phone.

Finally Reggie said that Suge was on the way. Then Tupac got pissed again, realizing that the festivities couldn't start until Suge actually arrived.

It was too much. Tyson was a friend and Tupac had his pride. Being made to wait like a medieval footman had happened once too often. Tupac decided to leave . . . just as Suge was arriving.

Greetings were exchanged. Seats were taken. The fight commenced. Tyson did his job quickly. "Tyson scored a knockout at 1:49 of the first round. The singing of the National Anthem lasted 41 seconds longer than the actual fight."

Then Suge, Tupac, and the crew went off to meet Tyson and congratulate him. But Tyson was taking too long so they left. On the way out of the MGM, Suge and Tupac slowed their movement until they could find, respectively, the rest of the Death Row posse and the Outlawz. Everybody was ready to get on the road and have a good time. And then one of Suge's posse, Travon Lane, hurried up alongside of Tupac and whispered in his right ear.

Tupac took off running. Big Frank zoomed off behind him, turned the corner, and couldn't believe his eyes as Tupac ran up to a guy and started throwing punches. The guy, Orlando Anderson, threw some punches too.

Punches continued to fly. A medallion that Tupac had recently purchased broke and fell to the floor. It was grabbed by Big Frank, who threw Tupac against the wall to get him away from the hail of flying fists. The rest of the Death Row crew continued to fight as muscle-bound Frank held his combative charge in place.

MGM security descended and the Death Row crew hurried back to the Luxor. And just as if nothing had happened, Tupac, Suge, and others discussed their next moves for the night. Tupac went up to his room, followed as always by Frank, who was more determined than ever to keep him safe. While waiting for Tupac to change, Frank fixed the medallion and saw something unusual. It wasn't the usual Death Row medallion but one that said Euphanasia on it, the name of Tupac's new production company. Disturbingly, there was also a black angel of death on it.

Once back downstairs, Tupac waited in valet parking for Suge, who finally showed. The ever-present groupies crowded around, beckoning, pleading, and urging Tupac and Suge to let them come along. No deal.

Tupac, Suge, and Frank started off for Suge's BMW when the rapper handed his keys to his bodyguard with new instructions. Frank was to drive the "little homies," the Outlawz, because the night was going to be a party night with much drinking and fun and somebody, Frank, had to be sober enough to drive them all back.

"What car do you want me to drive?" Frank asked.

"Drive Kidada's car," Tupac answered, adding that the "little homies" would take Frank to the car.

An entourage started to form. Suge, with Tupac in the BMW's front passenger seat, took off. Frank followed close behind as he was supposed to since he was the bodyguard on point.

Something was out of synch. Three to four more bodyguards should have been with them as they traveled to Suge's house before going down to the club for the after-party. But Big Frank didn't know the whole story. Approximately twenty security people that night had all been ordered down to the club. He was not just the only one watching over Tupac; from what he could discern he was the only security person on hand.

It wasn't adding up right. Frank didn't have his weapon since it was in *his* car. He didn't have any radio communications. Reggie Wright, who was always with Suge, was nowhere to be found . . . for whatever reason. To make matters worse, Kidada's car needed gas. The Outlawz noticed and warned him to get it handled.

Stopping was out of the question. He couldn't let Tupac out of his sight so he risked staying behind Suge. After all, they were only going to Suge's house and then to the club. Once there, the gas matter could be easily resolved. The warning light glowed bright and demanded Frank's attention. He stayed behind Suge and Tupac.

They spent around thirty minutes at Suge's house, horsing around and talking trash as they waited on him to change clothes. Finally Suge was ready and, with Tupac again in the BMW passenger seat and Frank following in Kidada's car, they rolled out.

An astonishing twenty to thirty vehicles were waiting to follow them as they hit the road back into town, ripping along at 70 to 80 miles per hour. Somehow, some way, Kidada's car hadn't run out of gas as they rolled back onto the Strip, which was jam-packed.

They waited near the Excalibur Hotel close to the Tropicana on the Strip. Suge and Tupac in the Beamer, directly in front of Frank, had turned their music up to thunder. A bicycle cop came over. Moments later, Suge got out of his car, walked to the back, and opened the trunk. The Beamer was new and didn't yet have a license plate. Were he and Tupac about to get busted?

The officer examined the trunk and let them go. They didn't go far or fast. On this fight night in Vegas, traffic was gridlocked. But it eventually let up and the cars moved on down the Strip.

At the next intersection they waited at a light. Then a white Cadillac pulled up beside Suge's car on the passenger side next to Tupac. The gunman's arm came out the window and the sound of gunshots ripped through the night.

The world slowed and then stopped. Then it spun into hyperspin. Frank jumped out of Kidada's car, hurrying to see if Suge and Tupac were okay. As Frank's feet hit the pavement, Suge wheeled the Beamer around into a U-turn and roared down the street. Was Suge trying to get to a hospital? It was impossible to know, so Frank flew back to Kidada's car and followed.

But the tires had been shot on Suge's Beamer and it broke down; Frank arrived seconds later. Police officers arrived on the scene, followed by paramedics. Suge's new Beamer looked forlorn and useless. Crowds gathered. The police moved them back using yellow crime scene tape. Suge was on the ground with blood spurting up from his head.

"Let him up!" Frank commanded. "Let him up! He's part of the entourage!"

"Who are you?" asked a police officer.

"I'm the bodyguard."

They let him up.

Tupac was still in Suge's BMW, and emergency medical personnel and police officers tried to open the stubborn passenger-side door. Suge urged them to let him try. The door gave in to Suge's power.

The emergency workers gently took Tupac from the vehicle and lay him down on the ground beside the Beamer. Frank knelt beside him.

Tupac said, "Frank, I can't breathe."

"No man, you're okay," Frank insisted.

"I can't breathe. I can't breathe."

Then he took a deep breath, let out a sigh, and closed his eyes.

part five

BELOVED

forty-four

TOO HARD TO BELIEVE

Kidada Jones, whom Tupac Amaru Shakur loved and had planned on marrying before he was gunned down, recalled, "I knew we should've never gone to Vegas that night. I had a horrible feeling about it. I've gone over it in my mind a million times. It wasn't supposed to happen. We weren't supposed to be there." She remembered the terrible aftermath: "We were at the Luxor Hotel and he went to a party. He said, 'I'm not taking you. There's been a fight with a Crip and it's not safe. So you stay here.' So I waited in our suite for him to come back. I lay down and was going to sleep when I got a call. They said, 'Pac's been shot.' I was like, 'Okay.' He'd been shot five times before that. I said, 'Where was he hit? In the leg, an arm? No big deal.' When I got to the hospital they handed me a bag of bloody clothes and jewelry and told me, 'He had no blood pressure when he came in. He's had two blood transfusions and he is in the ICU hanging by a string.' I got a blanket from the hospital and circled the parking lot for nine hours. I said, 'There's no way he's gonna die. There's just no way.' I walked around there till the sun came up and I had to keep my head down because I felt like I was going to projectile-vomit all over the place. I wanted to explode, just come out of my skin. I was in complete physical shock. He died at 4:30 P.M. a few days after that. For a while afterward, I didn't want to be alive. I was on my back, literally on my back, for months."

Tupac's *Above the Rim* costar, Marlon Wayans, was hopeful but cautious when he heard about the shooting: "I saw Pac 20 minutes before he got shot. I saw Pac in Vegas about to get into the car. . . . We walked off and got into a cab and they got in the Beamers. We went on to another party and 20 minutes later we heard Pac got shot. My first reaction was, again? Then I thought, he's gonna be all right. . . . He got shot five times before." Days later when Tupac died, Wayans said, "I cried like my mother cried when Marvin Gaye died."

Upon hearing the news that Tupac had been shot, Jada wondered how bad the situation was. "I remember calling Afeni and saying Fay do I need to get on a plane right now and she said, 'Jada he's gonna be okay. You get here when you can.'"

After all, this was Tupac who'd been shot before. He'd surely be all right this time also. He was tougher than nails and had always bounced back like a cat with nine lives. But Tupac had only one life, and when it ended Jada knew it without a word being said: "My mother knocked on the hotel door. Will opened the door. As soon as I saw her face, I knew he was gone."

Jada was devastated.

Snoop Dogg "was at Warren G's house in the living room. . . . We kept getting a whole bunch of calls and pages. Somebody told us to turn on the news. We turned the news on. I drove down there to the hospital cuz I wanted to see my nigga and make sure he was straight. I'm thinking he was gonna make it. . . . I said a little prayer to him and held his hand and whispered at him. He didn't have no consciousness but I felt like my spirit and his spirit connected. I felt like he got it."

When he died a few days later, Snoop broke down and wept.

Shock G knew that Tupac had seen it coming. He'd spent so much time talking about how he'd die. He'd devoted a lot of attention to leaving a legacy of words in rhyme that would live long after his demise. Nevertheless, the news of Tupac's murder ripped out a piece of Shock G's center.

Finally Tupac was lying still.

The tragedy of Tupac was titanic. The issues that he'd rapped about—the dangerous streets, black-on-black violence, drug use, and police brutality—had seemingly merged into the reality of his life. On the surface, at first glance, there seemed little to learn from him.

Tupac was not the best MC in the rap game (that honor goes to Rakim), but he was a charismatic presence, a gifted actor, and a poet who is still very much alive in the public mind. The preoccupation with Tupac is poignant but not surprising.

During his life, he dominated headlines for all of the wrong and right reasons. It was impossible to not know about him and few were ambivalent toward him. They either adored the truth and hope of his early music or despised its raw nature and social indictment.

Shock G has said,

> That (East Coast/West Coast) beef was silly, stupid, unnecessary, petty bullshit and took up way too much space in the media in my opinion. Focusing on that so much, we weren't able to focus on many of the more righteous, intelligent, beautiful and fun things going on in hip-hop at the time. Pac wasn't trying to set off a national war like that, he was just in shock of being shot and incarcerated in New York after putting in so much heart-filled work on behalf of the struggle. Pac took on the United States government, the media, and the national police force, all in defense of us, the common people. So for us to turn around and let him down like that, and allow him to be shot, robbed and persecuted,

without any answers; it not only broke his heart but it left him
bitter and disillusioned. Notice the change in his lyrics, his laugh,
the innocence in his eyes, and most of all, his attitude in interviews
after the New York shooting, sentencing, and prison term.

Naturally, he abandoned the East Coast afterwards, and who
could blame him? From 1989 to 1994, Pac's "I don't give a fuck"
thing was just a slogan, an anthem to represent the many lost
oppressed souls of America and the world. After 1995, he really
didn't give a fuck. I knew 2pac the human being, who wrote
2Pacalypse Now and "Me Against the World," not the tortured
broken beast who wrote Makaveli. I don't recognize my friend
Tupac Shakur on Makaveli. That's someone else.

There will be many more films, books, and plays about Tupac. They
will secure his place in the pantheon of dual-natured heroes/antiheroes.

But Asha Bandele, a personal friend of the rapper says, "Was he
somebody who made mistakes? Yes. The biggest misconception is that
he was a thug. He was not a thug. He had poetry. He was like many a
black boy out here who had so much to offer the world. People see him
through this hazy lens."

Social commentator Nelson George summed up the difficulties people confronted in attempting to figure out Tupac: "The truth is, we are
all way more complex than we give ourselves credit for. Tupac couldn't
escape the gangsta lifestyle because it expressed an angry need to lash
out that was an essential part of his character. The dichotomy of Tupac
is that he was a gangsta with a deeply artistic soul."

Like a church bell calling worshipers to service, his voice had rung
out to America, imploring the people in troubled communities, like the
ones he knew too well, to wake up, see the reality around them, and realize that there had to be a better way. At the same time, he urged the well-

off, secure, and content to take note that they were sitting atop rumbling volcanoes of urban unrest.

And it wasn't like Pac didn't know. He'd seen the best and worst that life could offer.

So many people, then and now, were prepared to stigmatize and flush from sight those same neighborhoods and people where thugs worked their mischief in the midst of struggling families who were trying to survive. Children of intellectual talent were preyed upon by equally talented children of the night. The elderly and wise were too often caught in the gun crossfire of the brazen and foolish. Hardworking people stayed true to their values of honest, legal labor against a tide of others gathering wealth in the shadows.

The world that Tupac rapped about was as complex, inspiring, heartbreaking, calm, and dangerous as life itself. Pac ensured that the world did not just dismiss the hard streets from which he'd come. And he clued the smug and sanctimonious that their suburban heavens were often facades over their own brand of hell.

Who shot Tupac Shakur in Las Vegas? If anyone knows, they aren't talking. It was a professional hit. Well planned and executed. So, the correct question is who paid the shooter? Was it the gangsters that he befriended in New York before his stint in the penitentiary? There is no evidence that he had any further problems with them after his release. Was it Suge Knight? Ridiculous. There were bullets flying all around the inside of the death car. Suge Knight had no way of making absolutely sure that those bullets would not kill him instead. Orlando Anderson? No. The hit had to be paid for by someone with deep pockets. It had to have cost at least a million dollars.

Will the puzzle ever be solved? Perhaps it already has been. There is something called street justice and, if that was in operation, the whole issue was handled a long time ago.

Will Tupac's fans ever see someone stand trial for the crime? That is highly unlikely and we don't need to dwell on it. What we should do is make sure that the young people in our lives learn self-control, respect for human life, and that brains, charm, and hard work will help them reach their goals.

forty-five

GOODBYE

Quincy Jones says, "I'll never forget that when he made an appointment to meet me at the Bel-Air Hotel, he arrived promptly at ten, then left a message with the maitre d' that he'd be back in a suit and tie. He wanted to greet me respectfully, not just as an artist and entrepreneur but as the father of the woman he loved. This is the side of Tupac that the media and his fans never saw, because of the mythology of the gangsta pose. A collection of his poetry . . . *The Rose That Grew from Concrete,* reveals a tragic fear of being seen as 'soft' because of his avocation for writing, which he thought exposed his vulnerability."

Tupac wasn't Malcolm X or Dr. Evil. He was a highly intelligent artist and philosopher. The difficulty most people had in trying to understand him was deciphering the quality of his philosophy, not his art, because art is expected to be abstract. Those closest and dearest to him and his spirit attended memorial services in New York or gathered later on the beach in Malibu to say fond farewells.

In New York, Treach of Naughty by Nature wanted to set the record straight. He tearfully explained that "Pac wasn't no gangster. I rolled with Pac. We came up together. He was a soldier."

Russell Simmons would later admit in his memoir *Life and Def* that "Tupac was always great with me. Despite the gangsta image he cultivated, whenever I would run into him at the Bowery Bar in New York and other glamour spots, he always had love for me. I mean, I never even heard him raise his voice in my presence. Despite his rep for acting reckless, I never saw Tupac act crazy. I know this must sound like I'm in denial, but I'm being very frank."

Tupac's stepbrother Mopreme opined that "I don't think he realized how great he was. I don't think he fully realized how much people admired him."

On the beach at Malibu, Afeni and others who'd been close to Tupac in life scattered some of his ashes (the rest would be divided between Afeni's home in Lumberton, North Carolina, and Soweto, South Africa) into the sea.

Shock G was there. "We threw all the gifts in the ocean for him. We threw the chicken wings and the Hennessey and his favorite pictures. Everybody brought something. Everybody said a little something. We brought drums and bongos. We had fires burning. That was his funeral."

When the water took his ashes and his loved ones started to dry their tears, Leila Steinberg, who'd seen so much in Tupac so early, asked, "Could we have done more? Could we have said more? All of us shoulder some of the responsibility."

When asked if Tupac changed rap music in any way, Dr. William Jelani Cobb, assistant professor of history at Spelman College says, "Yes, tremendously. He really helped solidify that template of the sensitive thug that virtually all of the later star artists have been beholden to. That would include DMX, 50 Cent, Jay-Z and Ja-Rule. Eminem has also talked about the impact Pac had on him as an artist. Tupac exponentially increased the visibility of the music, helped open doors for rappers who also wanted to act and unfortunately, became the music's first tragic icon. For better or worse, those tragic icons—Hendrix, Dean, et al., live on through their art and help ensure that the art form itself lives on. And as time goes on they come to occupy an even more central space as their peers grow older. In a decade, he will be a symbol of the faded youth of the hip-hop generation."

All the while, he did everything in his power to escape the demons that the hood had left in him. By the time he was pronounced dead on September 13, 1996, Tupac Amaru Shakur had emblazoned his name onto America's cultural pantheon along with the likes of Jimmy Hendrix, Elvis Presley, and John Lennon.

He had become an American icon.

Asha Bandele, Tupac's friend and author of *The Prisoner's Wife*, said that "if nothing else, Tupac gifted America with the truth of what it was to be a black boy in America in the 1990s. Some of it was really ugly, some of it was really beautiful and all of it was really human."

Quincy Jones said: "If we had lost Oprah Winfrey at twenty-five, we would have lost a relatively unknown, local market TV anchorwoman. If Martin Luther King had died at twenty-five he would have been a local Baptist minister who had not yet arrived on the national scene. If we had lost Malcolm X at twenty-five, we would have lost a hustler named Detroit Red. And, for that matter, if I had left the world at twenty-five, we would have lost a trumpet player and aspiring composer—just a sliver of my eventual life potential."

ACKNOWLEDGMENTS

Although it's impossible to thank everyone who inspired, assisted, and guided a task as monumental as writing about the life and times of a controversial genius and visionary poetic messenger like Tupac Amaru Shakur, it nevertheless has to be done.

Eternal thanks go out from our hearts to Anita Diggs, whose extensive editorial work, brilliance, and grace were always welcome, as was her interest in and knowledge of rap artists of the 1980s and 90s. Likewise, much appreciation is sent to Asha Bandale and Angela Ardis, both of whom knew Tupac as a friend. Their willingness to share their memories proves not only that they are women of class and heart but that much love still exists in this world for Pac.

Special thanks also to Dr. Sonja Trent-Brown, assistant professor of psychology at Hope College in Holland, Michigan, who provided brilliant psychological profiles of Tupac. Dr. William Jelani Cobb, associate professor of history at Spelman College in Atlanta, Georgia, took the work to a higher level of critical analysis.

Thanks also to everyone who spoke off the record for helping us understand both the good and bad sides of Tupac. His words so often blew over the heads of the people who needed to hear them most. But Pac wrote many words and they're still flowing out to us years after his death. As it was then, so it is now. If we just took time to listen, we might finally understand . . . maybe.

BIBLIOGRAPHY

BOOKS

Alexander, Frank. *Got Your Back: Protecting Tupac in the World of Gangsta Rap*. St. Martin's Griffin, 2000.

Allen, James, et al. *Without Sanctuary: Lynching Photography in America*. Twin Palms Publishing, 2000.

Ambrose, Stephen E. *Rise to Globalism*. Penguin Books, 1988.

Ardis, Angela. *Inside a Thug's Heart*. Kensington Books, 2004.

Baldwin, James. *The Fire Next Time*. Dell Publishing, 1963.

Bastfield, Darrin Keith. *Back in the Day*. Da Capo, 2002.

Bell, Derrick. *And We Are Not Saved: The Elusive Quest for Racial Justice*. Basic Books, 1987.

Brown, Elaine. *A Taste of Power: A Black Woman's Story*. Pantheon Books, 1992.

Chang, Jeff. *Can't Stop, Won't Stop*. St. Martin's Press, 2005.

Churchill, Ward, and Jim Vander Wall. *The COINTELPRO Papers: Documents from the FBI's Secret Wars Against the Dissent in the United States*. South End Press, 1990.

———. *Agents of Repression: The FBI's Secret War Against the Black Panthers and the American Indian Movement*. South End Press, 1990.

Clark-Hine, Darlene, et al. *The African American Odyssey*. Prentice-Hall, 2003.

Coker, Cheo Hodari. *Unbelievable*. Three Rivers Press, 2003.

Dogg, Snoop. *The Doggfather*. William Morrow, 1999.

Douglass, Frederick. *Narrative of the Life of Frederick Douglass.* Dover, 1995.

Dyson, Michael Eric. *Holler If You Hear Me.* Basic Civitas, 2001.

Ferrell, Robert H. *American Diplomacy: A History.* 3rd ed. Norton, 1975.

Foner, Philip S. *The Black Panthers Speak.* Da Capo Press, 1970.

Forkos, Heather. *Tupac Shakur.* Chelsea House, 1998.

George, Nelson. *Hip-Hop America.* Penguin Books, 1998.

Gray, Fred D. *Bus Ride to Justice: Changing the System by the System.* New South Books, 2002.

Guy, Jasmine. *Afeni Shakur: The Evolution of a Revolutionary.* Atria Books, 2004.

Haley, Alex. *The Autobiography of Malcolm X.* One World, 1965.

Haskins, Jim. *Power to the People: The Rise and Fall of the Black Panther Party.* Simon & Schuster, 1997.

Hayes, Floyd W. *A Turbulent Voyage: Readings in African American Studies.* North Carolina State University Press, 2000.

Heller, Jerry. *Ruthless: A Memoir.* Simon Spotlight Entertainment, 2005.

Hilliard, David, and Lewis Cole. *This Side of Glory: The Autobiography of David Hilliard and the Story of the Black Panther Party.* Little, Brown, 1993.

Hilliard, David, and Donald Weise. *Huey P. Newton Reader.* Seven Stories Press, 2002.

Jones, Charles E. *The Black Panther Party (Reconsidered).* Black Classic Press, 1998.

Jones, Quincy. *The Autobiography of Quincy Jones.* Doubleday, 2001.

———. *Tupac Shakur, 1971–1996.* Three Rivers Press, 1996.

Joseph, Jamal. *Tupac Shakur: Legacy.* Atria, 2006.

Katznelson, Ira. *When Affirmative Action Was White: An Untold History of Racial Inequality in Twentieth-Century America.* Norton, 2005.

Kitwana, Bakari. *The Hip-Hop Generation.* Civitas Books, 2002.

Kluger, Richard. *Simple Justice: The History of Brown v. Board of Education and Black America's Struggle for Equality.* Random House, 1975.

LaFeber, Walter. *The American Age: U.S. Foreign Policy at Home and Abroad.* Norton, 1994.

Leuchtenburg, William. *In the Shadow of FDR: From Harry Truman to George W. Bush.* Cornell University Press, 2001.

Morris, Aldon. *Origins of the Civil Rights Movement.* Free Press, 1984.

Nash, Gary. *Red, White, and Black: The Peoples of Early North America.* Prentice-Hall, 2005.

Ogbar, Jeffrey O.G. *Black Power: Radical Politics and the African American Identity.* Johns Hopkins University Press, 2004.

Puzo, Mario. *The Godfather.* Putnam, 1969.

Quinn, Eithne. *Nuthin' but a "G" Thang.* Columbia University Press, 2005.

Ro, Ronin. *Bad Boy: The Influence of Sean "Puffy" Combs on the Music Industry.* Pocket Books, 2001.

———. *The Biography of Dr. Dre.* Thunder's Mouth Press, 2007.

———. *Have Gun Will Travel.* Broadway Books, 1998.

Sandy, Candace, and Dawn Marie Daniels. *How Long Will They Mourn Me.* Ballantine, 2006.

Scott, Cathy. *The Killing of Tupac Shakur.* Huntington Press, 1997.

Shields, Charles J. *Mockingbird: A Portrait of Harper Lee.* Henry Holt, 2006.

Storey, William. *U.S. Government and Politics.* Edinburgh University Press, 2007.

Sullivan, Randall. *Labyrinth.* Grove Press, 2002.

Toobin, Jeffrey. *The Nine: Inside the Secret World of the Supreme Court.* Doubleday, 2007.

Touré. *never drank the kool-aid.* Picador, 2006,

Walker, David. *David Walker's Appeal, to the Coloured Citizens of the World but in Particular, and Very Expressly, to Those of the United States of America.* Black Classics Press, 1993.

Watkins, S. Craig. *Hip-Hop Matters.* Beacon Press, 2005.

Weems, Clenora Hudson. *Emmett Till: The Sacrificial Lamb of the Civil Rights Movement.* Bedford Publishers, 1994.

Wiese, Andrew. *Places of Their Own: African American Suburbanization in the Twentieth Century.* University of Chicago Press, 2004.

Williams, Bruce. *Rollin' with Dre: An Insider's Tale of the Rise, Fall, and Rebirth of West Coast Hip-Hop.* One World, 2008.

Wright, Bruce. *Black Robes, White Justice.* Carol Publishing Group, 1987.

Zimroth, Peter. *Perversion of Justice: The Prosecution and Acquittal of the Panther 21.* Viking Press, 1974.

Zinn, Howard. *A People's History of the United States.* New Press, 2003.

JOURNAL ARTICLES

Henderson, Errol A. "The Lumpenproletariat as Vanguard? The Black Panther Party, Social Transformation, and Pearson's Analysis of Huey P. Newton." *Journal of Black Studies* 28, no. 2 (November 1997).

Myer, Philip. "Aftermath of Martyrdom: Negro Militancy and Martin Luther King." *Public Opinion Quarterly* 33, no. 2 (Summer 1969).

Sandarg, Robert. "Jean Genet and the Black Panther Party." *Journal of Black Studies* 16, no. 3 (March 1986).

MAGAZINE ARTICLES

Anson, Robert. "To Die Like a Gangsta." *Vanity Fair*, March 1997.

Bruck, Connie. "The Takedown of Tupac." *New Yorker*, July 7, 1997.

Powell, Kevin. "The Short Life and Violent Death of Tupac Shakur." *Rolling Stone*, October 31, 1996.

NEWSPAPER ARTICLES

Barron, James. "Rapper Becomes Victim." *New York Times*, December 1, 1994.

Britt, Donna. "A Little Poetic Justice." *Atlanta Journal and Constitution*, November 8, 1993.

Gladwell, Malcolm. "Shakur Goes Free Pending Appeal." *Washington Post*, October 14, 1995.

Murray, Sonia. "Tupac's Mama." *Atlanta Journal and Constitution*, May 28, 1995.

Philips, Chuck. "Q&A with Tupac Shakur." *Los Angeles Times*, October 25, 1995.

Touré. "Biggie Smalls, Rap's Man of the Year." *New York Times*, December 18, 1994.

DOCUMENTARIES

1997: *Tupac Shakur: Thug Immortal*
1997: *Tupac Shakur: Words Never Die* (TV)
2001: *Tupac Shakur: Before I Wake*
2001: *Welcome to Death Row*

2002: *Thug Angel: The Life of an Outlaw*
2002: *Biggie & Tupac*
2002: *The Westside*
2003: *2Pac 4 Ever*
2003: *Tupac: Resurrection* (Nominated for an Academy Award)
2004: *Tupac: The Hip-Hop Genius* (TV)
2006: *So Many Years, So Many Tears*
2007: *Tupac Revelation*
2008: *Notorious* (TV)

WEBSITES

www.npr.org
www.npr.org/templates/story/story.php?storyId=19105520
www.africanaonline.com/malcom_x.htm
http://afroamhistory.about.com/library/blmaria_stewart_religion.htm
http://digital.nypl.org/schomburg/writers_aa19/bio2.html
www.yale.edu/lawweb/avalon/treatise/king/mlk01.htm
www.africanaonline.com/orga_black_panther.htm
www.pbs.org/hueypnewton/people/people_hoover.html
www.pbs.org/johngardner/chapters/5a.html
www.cnn.com/SPECIALS/cold.war/episodes/13/documents/lbj
www.thenation.com/doc/20030217/staub
www.stopbeingfamous.com
www.stanford.edu/group/King/additional_resources/articles/mercury.htm
www.senate.gov/artandhistory/history/common/generic/VP_Spiro_
    Agnew.htm
www.infoplease.com/spot/affirmative1.html
www.whitehouse.gov/history/presidents/rr40.html
www.pbs.org/wgbh/amex/carter/peopleevents/e_1980.html
http://nymag.com/nymetro/news/bizfinance/columns/
    bottomline/n_9352
www.americanrhetoric.com/MovieSpeeches/moviespeechwallstreet.html
http://eightiesclub.tripod.com/id316.htm
www.usatoday.com/news/washington/2004-06-10-tolliver-vignette_
    x.htm

www.washingtonmonthly.com/features/2003/0309.mendacity
-index.htm

http://frontpagemag.com/articles/Read.aspx?GUID=3362356F-98D0
-4CC9-A24C-27D5F97544EF

http://socialjustice.ccnmtl.columbia.edu/index.php/Republic_of_New_
Afrika

www.geocities.com/southernscene/edu3.html

www.boston.com/news/globe/ideas/articles/2003/10/19/return_of_
the_weathermen

www.nationmaster.com/encyclopedia/Mutulu-Shakur

www.time.com/time/specials/2007/
article/0,28804,1709148_1709143_1709668,00.html

www.ferris.edu/jimcrow/menu.htm

www.vatican.va/holy_father/john_paul_ii/messages/peace/documents/
hf_jp-ii_mes_19891208_xxiii-world-day-for-peace_en.html

www.bookrags.com/biography/manuel-a-noriega/4.html

www.globalsecurity.org/military/ops/just_cause.htm

www.globalsecurity.org/military/ops/desert_shield.htm

http://archives.cnn.com/2002/US/04/28/la.riot.anniversary/

www.rollingstone.com/reviews/movie/5947337/review/5947338/
jungle_fever

www.arlingtoncemetery.net/tmarsh.htm

http://query.nytimes.com/gst/fullpage.html?res=9D0CE4DD163CF93
BA15755C0A967958260&sec=&spon=&pagewanted=all

www.notablebiographies.com/St-Tr/Thomas-Clarence.html

http://people.virginia.edu/~ybf2u/Thomas-Hill/timeline-text.html

www.amren.com/ar/2000/10/

www.norfolk.gov/About/20th_century.asp

www.vahistorical.org/civilrights/massiveresistance.htm#38

www.vcdh.virginia.edu/reHIST604/images/1957a.jpg

www.nsu.edu/norfolk17

www.ci.lumberton.nc.us/index.asp?Type=NONE&SEC=%7BB755998
D-C360-4407-96DC-F7D5075B51F8%7D

www.britannica.com/eb/article-9049334/Lumberton

www.co.robeson.nc.us/hist.htm

www.lumbeetribe.com/lumbee/timeline.htm

www.trutv.com/library/crime/gangsters_outlaws/outlaws/dillinger/
  1.html
www.filmsite.org/crimefilms.html
www.lib.unc.edu/ncc/ref/nchistory/mar2008/index.html
http://www.achievement.org/autodoc/page/jon0bio-1
www.alleyezonme.com/2pacarticles/tupacshakur/9/This_Thugs_Life.
  html
http://encarta.msn.com/encyclopedia_761593238/amar%C3%BA_
  tupac.html
www.jqjacobs.net/andes/tupac_amaru.html
www.wikipedia.com
www.apnmag.com/summer_2006/Clinton%20Correctional%20Facility
  .php
www.prisonsociety.org/about/history.shtml
http://weblogs.newsday.com/sports/boxing/blog/2008/03/tupac_and_
  tyson.html

DISCOGRAPHY

After Tupac died, the executors of his estate went through his crates and tapes of material and released a lot of it that he probably never wanted the world to hear. *Those CDs are not included here.*

ALBUMS

This Is an EP Release. Tommy Boy Records (recording debut with Digital Underground), 1991.

2Pacalypse Now. Interscope Records, 1991.

Strictly 4 My N.I.G.G.A.Z. Interscope Records, 1993.

Poetic Justice. Epic Records, 1993. Soundtrack.

Thug Life. Interscope Records, 1994.

Above the Rim. Death Row Records, 1994. Soundtrack.

Me Against the World. Interscope Records, 1995.

One Million Strong. Mergela Records, 1995.

All Eyez on Me. Death Row Records, 1996.

Makaveli: The Don Killuminati: The 7 Day Theory. Death Row Records, 1996.

Gridlock'd. Death Row Records, 1997. Soundtrack.

Gang Related. Death Row Records, 1997. Soundtrack.

TOP 10 BILLBOARD SINGLES

| 1991 | "Brenda's Got a Baby" |
| 1991 | "If My Homie Calls" |

1993   "I Get Around"
1993   "Keep Ya Head Up"
1995   "Dear Mama"
1995   "Old School"
1995   "Me Against the World"
1995   "So Many Tears"
1996   "California Love"
1996   "Hit Em Up"
1996   "How Do U Want It"

FILMOGRAPHY

1991 *Nothing but Trouble* (Warner Bros.); (One of Tupac's earliest screen appearances, he appeared with Shock G and the Digital Underground; they also collaborated in making the film's soundtrack); directed by Dan Akroyd; produced by Lester Berman and Peter K. Weiss; starring Chevy Chase, Dan Akroyd, John Candy, and Demi Moore.

1992 *Juice* (Paramount Pictures); (Tupac played the part of Bishop); directed by Ernest R. Dickerson; produced by Peter Frankfurt, David Heyman, and Neal H. Moritz; starring Tupac Shakur, Omar Epps, Jermaine Hopkins, Khalil Kain, and Cindy Herron.

1993 *Poetic Justice* (Columbia Pictures); (Tupac played the part of Lucky); directed by John Singleton; produced by John Singleton; starring Tupac Shakur, Janet Jackson, Regina King, Joe Torry, and Tyra Ferrell.

1994 *Above the Rim* (New Line Cinema); (Tupac played the part of Birdie); directed by Jeff Pollack; produced by Bunny Medina; starring Duane Martin, Leon (a.k.a, Leon Robinson), Tupac Shakur, David Bailey, and Tonya Pinkins.

1995 *Bullet* (New Line Home Video); (Tupac played the part of Tank); directed by Julien Temple; produced by Graham Burke and Gary Coote; starring Tupac Shakur and Mickey Rourke.

1997 *Gridlock'd* (Universal Pictures); (Tupac played the part of Ezekiel "Spoon" Whitmore); directed by Vondie Curtis-Hall; produced by Michael Bennett; starring Tupac Shakur, Tim Roth, and Thandie Newton.

1997 *Gang Related* (Orion Pictures/MGM); (Tupac played the part of Jake Rodriguez); directed by Jim Kouf; produced by Steven Stabler; starring Tupac Shakur, James Belushi, Lela Rochon, Dennis Quaid, and James Earl Jones.

INDEX

B
03/22/2011   3CLY0019866
SHA

McQuillar, Tayannah
Tupac Shakur

DATE DUE			

DEMCO